THE HISTORY OF COMPUTERS

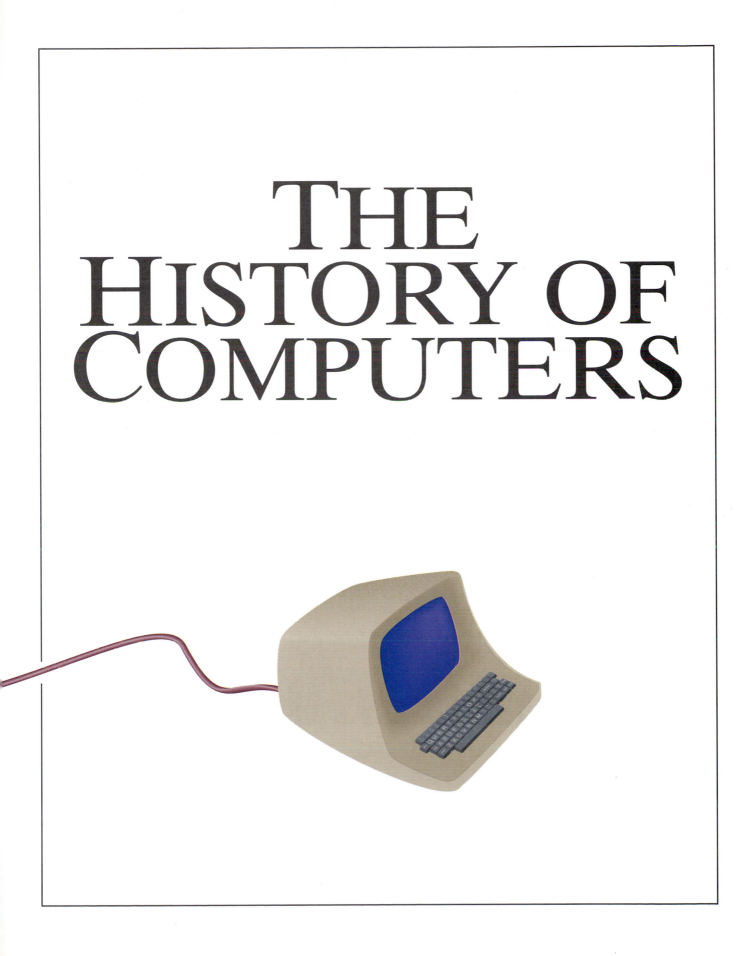

THE HISTORY OF COMPUTERS

LES FREED

Illustrated by
SARAH ISHIDA

Ziff-Davis Press
Emeryville, California

Development Editor	Valerie Haynes Perry
Copy Editor	Kelly Green
Project Coordinator	Barbara Dahl
Cover Design and Illustration	Regan Honda
Book Design	Carrie English
Illustrator	Sarah Ishida
Contributing Artists	Carrie English, Daniel Clark, and Cherie Plumlee
Word Processing	Howard Blechman
Page Layout	M.D. Barrera
Cover copy	Valerie Haynes Perry
Indexer	Carol Burbo

Ziff-Davis Press books are produced on a Macintosh computer system with the following applications: FrameMaker®, Microsoft® Word, QuarkXPress®, Adobe Illustrator®, Adobe Photoshop®, Adobe Streamline™, MacLink®*Plus*, Aldus® FreeHand™, Collage Plus™.

If you have comments or questions or would like to receive a free catalog, call or write:
Ziff-Davis Press
5903 Christie Avenue
Emeryville, CA 94608
1-800-688-0448

ISBN 1-56276-275-3

Manufactured in the United States of America
♲ This book is printed on paper that contains 50% total recycled fiber of which 20% is de-inked postconsumer fiber.
10 9 8 7 6 5 4 3 2 1

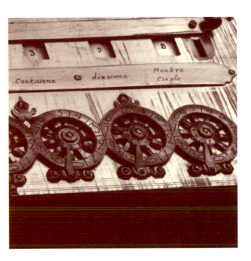

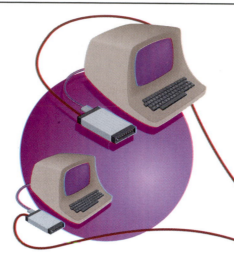

At the 1984 introduction of Apple's Macintosh computer, Steve Jobs of Apple Computer predicted that the personal computer would become a common household appliance, much like a toaster or a television set. Jobs's remark was laughed at by a large portion of the computer industry, particularly by people who worked for companies that made large, expensive mainframe computer systems. Computers, the naysayers said, were too expensive and too complex to appeal to the average Joe or Jane.

The naysayers were right—to a point. The computers *they* were building were in fact too expensive and complex for most people. Jobs, with Apple cofounder Steve Wozniak, helped to start a revolution that set the entire computer industry on its ear. In the space of ten short years, personal computers outnumbered mainframe computers by a factor of thousands. In the interim, many mainframe computer manufacturers went the way of the brachiosaurus, taking the naysayers—and their slow, lumbering, oversized, and overpriced computers—with them.

I think toasters still outnumber PCs (research data on this kind of thing is hard to find), but today you can walk into virtually any Target, Wal-Mart, or Sears store and find computers for sale, a few aisles over from the toasters, food processors, and drip coffeemakers. Many households and virtually all businesses now have one or more personal computers, with millions more being sold every year.

Thanks to an abundance of cheap computing power, we routinely do things that seemed like science fiction just 15 years ago. Our kids do their homework on computers. Business people use them for word processing, number crunching, inventory tracking, billing, check writing, and a thousand other functions. Computers guide the Space Shuttle, monitor air and water pollution, and help design more fuel-efficient automobiles. Computers control critical life-support and diagnostic imaging equipment in hospitals. They also control automobile antilock braking systems that help keep many of us out of the hospital.

This book was designed to help people understand how computers came to be. The book progresses chronologically, but you can jump around and read it in any order you like. Because this is an historical book, I have focused on the significance of the topics covered, and not necessarily on the deep technical details of each topic. If, after reading this book, you'd like to know more about the inner workings of computers, pick up a copy of Ron White's *How Computers Work*, also published by Ziff-Davis Press.

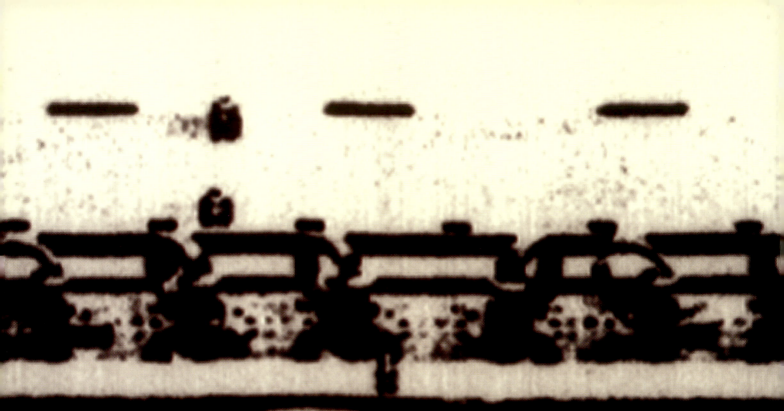
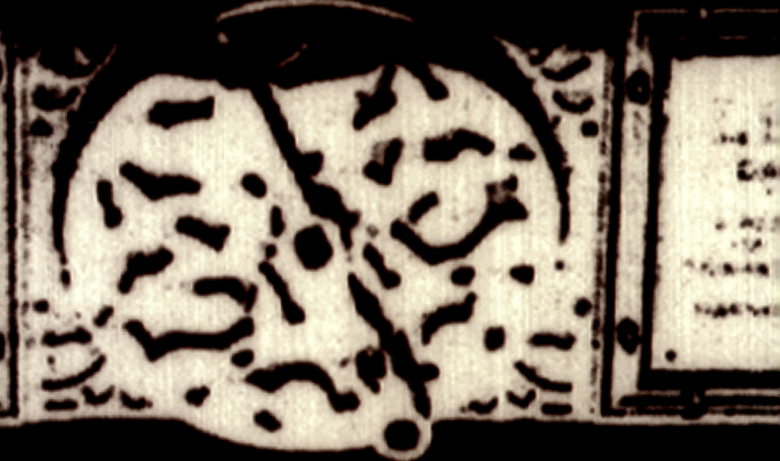

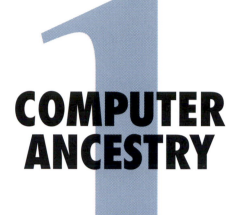

COMPUTER ANCESTRY

CONTENTS

AS I WRITE these first words of this book, I'm sitting on a sofa in my office, laptop computer literally on my lap. By today's standards, this particular laptop is nothing special—just a midrange model with a 33-megahertz 80486 processor, 4 megabytes of memory, and a 180-megabyte hard disk. By the standards of 100, 50, or even 10 years ago, it is a piece of magic.

A few days before I started work on this book, my computer and I visited the National Museum of Science and Industry in London. The museum has one of the world's best collections of early calculating machines and computers. If computers had feelings, my laptop would have felt like you or I might feel if we bumped into Cro-Magnon man while out walking the dog. Those early machines were as different from today's computers as a Roman chariot is from a Corvette.

In their day, these early calculators were cutting edge, high-tech stuff. But the technology was that of brass gears and levers, a far cry from the silicon semiconductors of today's machines. Many of the early machines never really worked as promised, and the most famous—Charles Babbage's Analytical Engine—couldn't be built with the technology of the day.

I've chosen to include these early machines in the book because they show just how far and how fast we've come. The first mechanical computer (Schickard's calculator) appeared in 1623. When Charles Babbage died in 1871—almost 250 years after the first calculating machine appeared—he was still working on his all-mechanical Analytical Engine. It would be another 70 years before engineers would learn how to build an all-electronic computer.

Technology certainly limited the advance in the state of computing for those 300-odd years, but there just wasn't much demand for calculating machines. Day-to-day life in the premodern world didn't require much mathematical knowledge, and even well-educated people didn't necessarily know much math beyond simple addition and subtraction. Mathematics was the province of scientists, particularly those working in the physical sciences of physics and astronomy. For those scientists, calculation was an endless chore.

It is no surprise that most of the early calculating machines were constructed by scientists in an attempt to ease the constant burden of calculcation. Mathematical facts that we take for granted—the value of π or the sine of 45 degrees, for example—required hours of laborious longhand calculation. Then as now, astronomers and scientists could look up those facts in books of tables, but the tables were notoriously error prone. Rather than risk an expensive and time-consuming experiment to the vagaries of a book of tables, most scientists preferred to perform their own calculations.

The lack of a large market for their wares combined with the difficulty and expense of building these machines resulted in very few being built. Babbage, in fact, never finished his Analytical Engine, but a working copy was built by IBM in the 1950s. We are fortunate that most of the early calculators have been preserved for us to wonder at today.

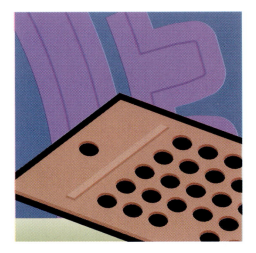

CHAPTER 1

Early Mechanical Calculators

WHO BUILT THE first computer? The answer depends on what you call a computer. The first mechanical calculating devices were built in the early seventeenth century. While they weren't computers in the true sense of the word—they could only perform a limited number of mathematical functions, and often didn't do that very well—they represented the first attempts to mechanize the task of computation.

As the seventeenth century began, the world was undergoing some very radical changes. Galileo (1564–1642) had proven that the Earth was not the center of the universe as previously thought. His perfection of the telescope set off a new wave of interest in astronomy, a science that often requires precise and laborious calculations.

Prior to the seventeenth century, the voyages of Columbus and Magellan in the fifteenth and sixteenth centuries had proven that the Earth was in fact a sphere, and that there was a great deal more to the planet than Europe, Africa, and the Far East. These developments caused the seafaring European nations—England, France, and Spain in particular—to set out to colonize the New World. Like astronomy, navigation also requires precise calculations. An incorrect navigational calculation could easily send a ship far off course or aground, and an incorrect tidal calculation could leave a ship "high and dry."

Before the arrival of calculating machines, navigators, astronomers, bankers, and scientists relied on books of tables for their calculations. The numbers in the tables were calculated by hand, and the results were typeset and printed. But the books of tables had their own set of problems. Because they were calculated by humans, they were subject to human error. The process of transcription and typesetting introduced additional errors. Obviously, a better way had to be found.

Several great seventeenth-century mathematicians, such as Blaise Pascal and Gottfried Wilhelm Leibniz, set out to automate the process of calculation. Their mechanical calculators could perform basic mathematical functions—addition, subtraction, multiplication, and division—with fairly good accuracy and speed. Still, their machines were delicate, difficult to build, and slow to use. Even when used to aid in the compilation of tables, the early machines still required that the results be copied down by hand—with the attendant chance of introducing errors. As a result, their commercial appeal was limited, and relatively few were built. While several inventors improved on these early designs, the state of the art of computing machinery didn't improve much for nearly 200 years.

At the beginning of the nineteenth century, England was in the midst of the first Industrial Revolution. As the Industrial Revolution progressed, the need for accurate computations became more acute. In 1822, a young English astronomy student named Charles Babbage (1792–1871) wrote a scientific paper entitled "On the Theoretical Principles of the Machinery for Calculating Tables." In the paper, Babbage proposed to build a machine called the Difference Engine to mechanize the production of tables. The machine would use "the unerring certainty of mechanism" to assure that the calculations were error free, and the machine would also print its results directly on paper, thus eliminating the additional errors introduced by typesetting.

Babbage's paper was well received by the Royal Astronomical Society, and the Society took the then unusual step of recommending that the English government provide funds for Babbage to continue his research. The government agreed and gave Babbage a sizable grant for the times (£17,000) so he could build his Difference Engine. Unfortunately, Babbage had grossly underestimated the complexity involved in constructing such a machine. To make matters worse, he was a relentless perfectionist, and insisted that each of the three-ton machine's 25,000 parts fit together with extreme precision.

In 1827, Babbage suffered a nervous breakdown, due in no small part to his obsession with the Difference Engine. In 1833, he abandoned work on the machine, having exhausted his grant money. At that point, the unfinished (yet partially functional) Difference Engine consisted of over 2,000 hand-made brass parts. He attempted to gain additional government financing in 1842, but was repeatedly turned down.

Undaunted, Babbage carried on and even expanded his work. During the hiatus in work on the Difference Engine, Babbage conceived of his Analytical Engine. While the Difference Engine was essentially a very large calculator, the Analytical Engine would be a programmable machine—capable of storing programs, performing mathematical operations, and using punched cards for storage, input, and output. The engine would have separate processing and storage units (called *the mill* and *the store*), and would be capable of conditional branching—the ability to choose from a number of alternative courses of action, depending on the state of the machine at a particular point in time.

Circa 1833, Babbage began work on the Analytical Engine, often stealing parts from the unfinished Difference Engine. The Analytical Engine was still unfinished when he died in 1871. His son, Henry Prevost Babbage, carried on his father's work intermittently for many years. Henry completed a small portion of the Analytical Engine in 1910, which was when the machine was used to calculate the value of π to 20 decimal places (although it could only print out the value to seven decimal places). Unfortunately, the calculations from this machine were later found to contain errors—perhaps the first recorded case of computer error.

Although Babbage did not live to see it, his work had a lasting impact on computing technology. Babbage's use of punched cards as a storage device was prophetic—by about 100 years. The concepts of separate storage and computation units persist to this day, and all modern computers perform conditional branching.

Mechanical Calculators Developed in the 1600s

Early calculators of the seventeenth century represent some of the first attempts to mechanize the task of mathematical calculation. Invented before the advent of mass production techniques, each machine was built entirely by hand.

The Science Museum/Science & Society Picture Library

Pascal's *Pascaline* Calculator (1642) Blaise Pascal (1623–1662) designed and built this machine at the age of 19. Pascal is thought to have designed the machine as an aid to computation for his father, who was a tax collector. To use this calculator, the user dialed in numbers on the wheels using a stylus. The numbers in the windows at the top of the machine changed to show the answer to the problem. To add numbers, the user turned the wheels clockwise; to subtract, the wheels were turned counterclockwise.

| 1660 | 1610 | 1620 | 1630 | 1640 | **1642** | 1650 |

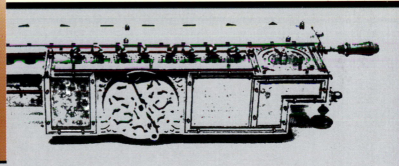

The Science Museum/Science & Society Picture Library

The Leibniz Wheel (1673)
Built by Gottfried Wilhelm Leibniz (1646–1716), this was the first all-metal machine that could perform addition, subtraction, multiplication, and division. The heart of the machine was a device called the Leibniz Wheel. The wheel formed the basis of most modern-day mechanical adding machines.

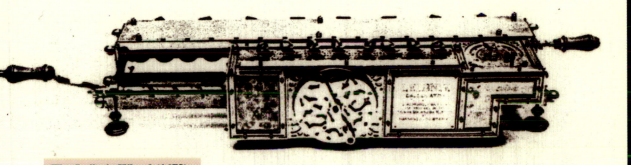

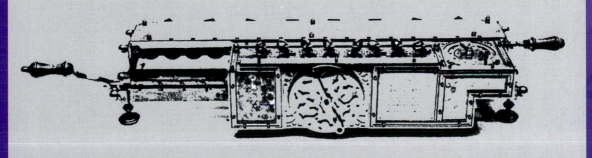

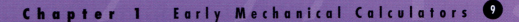

| 1660 | 1670 | **1673** | 1680 | 1690 | 1700 | 1710 |

Charles Babbage's Calculating Engines

Although he was a man of many talents, Charles Babbage (1792–1871) is best known for his two calculating machines, the Difference Engine and the Analytical Engine. Neither of these two machines were finished in his lifetime, yet they both had a lasting impact on virtually every calculating and computing machine that followed.

Babbage's Difference Engine #1 (1832)
Although Babbage never completed the entire machine, this portion of the Difference Engine #1 was completed in 1832. It contains 2,000 handmade brass parts. It is still in working order, and was the first completely automatic calculating device. The entire machine, had it been completed, would have contained about 25,000 parts and would have weighed 3 tons.

1770   1780   1790   1880   1820   1830 **1832** 1840

Babbage's Difference Engine #2 (1852)   This machine was an improved version of Babbage's original design. It is simpler and more elegant in its operation than Engine #1, and was designed to be easier to build. Babbage offered this design to the English government in 1852—perhaps as a way of repaying their faith in his earlier efforts. The first working version (and it works error free) of this machine was built by dedicated members of the Science Museum in London between 1989 and 1991.

Babbage's Analytical Engine (1910)   The most ambitious of Babbage's designs was never completed. The only working model of the Analytical Engine is this partial working model, completed by Babbage's son Henry in 1910—some 39 years after his father's death. At a demonstration in 1910, this machine calculated the value of π to 20 decimal places—but the results from this machine were later found to be in error.

A Punched Card
Babbage's use of punched cards in computation was an invention that was about 100 years ahead of its time.

1850 **1852** 1860   1870   1880   1890   1900   **1910**

The First Robot: Jacquard's Loom

VIRTUALLY ALL COMPUTERS—modern or antique—require some form of data storage medium. Data storage media contain the input and output data from the computer as well as the program to be performed by the computer. Modern-day storage media include floppy disks, hard disks, and semiconductor memory chips. You may be surprised to learn that Jacquard's loom, the first data storage mechanism, actually predates the first official computer.

Joseph Marie Jacquard (1752–1834) was a man of many talents. His first display of inventiveness came in 1770 when, at the age of 18, he built a machine to automate the production of knife blades. On the morning of the machine's trial run, his co-workers—fearful that the machine would put them out of work—smashed the machine to bits.

After the less-than-warm reception given his machine, Jacqard left the knife foundry in his native Lyons, France and became a typesetter's apprentice and printer. Printing was one of the few mechanized industries of the day, and Jacquard quickly learned how to operate, repair, and in several cases improve the machinery. But the death of this father—a fabric weaver—in 1790 brought him back to his family home in Lyons.

Lyons was, at that time, one of the silk-weaving capitals of the world. As a small boy, Jacquard had worked in the silk looms there as a drawboy. Drawboys moved the warp threads back and forth across the loom, putting the warp thread above certain longitudinal threads and below others, thus creating an intricate pattern in the weave. A single mistake could ruin the entire fabric.

After his father's death, Jacquard found himself with a house, two looms, and a little money. Remembering the long hours he had spent at the loom as a child, he decided to use his newfound knowledge of machines to build a better loom. Specifically, he wanted to automate the placement of the warp threads in the loom, thus eliminating the need for the drawboy. If this could be done, the amount of handwork would be greatly reduced, and the entire weaving process would be much faster and error free.

Years earlier, the French inventor Jacques de Vaucanson (1709–1782) had built a loom similar to the one that Jacquard envisioned. De Vaucanson had solved the drawboy problem, and had built a loom that used a series of perforated wooden cards to control the loom. By varying the pattern of the holes in the cards, de Vaucanson's loom could generate varieties of complicated patterns with very little human intervention. Unfortunately, de Vaucanson's machine had not been a commercial success, and the machine had been misplaced.

Jacquard set out to reinvent de Vaucanson's loom during the mid-1770s, working on the machine on and off for over 20 years. His work was interrupted by the French Revolution, and Jacquard served as a soldier on the side of the revolution. Returning to Lyons after the war, he once again immersed himself in his work.

In 1801, Napoleon's government offered a reward of 10,000 francs for a machine that could weave fishing nets. Jacquard had already built such a machine, and he sent it to Paris. Jacquard received a medal and the reward. He was also given the job of curator of the French National Museum of Arts and Industry. There, in an attic of the museum's storage room, he found de Vaucanson's loom.

The de Vaucanson loom, as Jacquard had heard, used a series of punched cards to guide the warp threads. But the machine was too complicated to be practical (de Vaucanson was famous for his incredibly complex inventions) and it was limited to very small patterns. When Jacquard returned to Lyons a few years later, he returned to work on his loom, this time armed with de Vaucanson's ideas.

Jacquard quickly perfected his loom and circa 1804, the French Silkmaking Commission voted to adopt the machine as a standard. The French silkworkers had other ideas. Jacquard's machine required only one operator as opposed to two. Use of the loom also eliminated the drawboy, and many weavers had come to count on the extra income provided by employing their children as drawboys. Hostility towards Jacquard and his machine built to a boil. Several attempts were made on his life, but each time he was saved by police intervention. In 1806, Napoleon declared Jacquard's patents to be public property. In return, Jacquard was given the modest sum of 3,000 francs for each machine sold. By 1812, there were over 11,000 Jacquard looms in use; in 1834, the year of Jacquard's death, there were 30,000 in use in Jacquard's hometown of Lyons. Use of the Jacquard loom spread worldwide, and Jacquard's basic design is still in use today.

De Vaucanson and Jacquard's punched cards took on a life of their own. Charles Babbage proposed to use them as the controlling mechanism of his Analytical Engine. Many years later, an American named Herman Hollerith would use punched cards to build an empire named International Business Machines (IBM).

The Jacquard Loom

Good ideas never die, and the punched card is living proof of that fact. The idea of storing information on punched paper or wood was first conceived by French inventor Jacques de Vaucanson in the 1740s. Like Jacquard, de Vaucanson used the cards to store the pattern for an automated loom. De Vaucanson's loom was not a commercial success, and Jacquard's later improvements to de Vaucanson's loom revolutionized the fabric industry. The Jacquard loom caught the eye of a young Charles Babbage, and Babbage's unfinished Analytical Engine was designed to use punched cards for data and program storage.

Jacquard's Loom In fabric weaving, a pattern is created in the fabric by running the warp (cross) thread either over or under the longitudinal threads. Each warp thread must cross a different combination of threads. Before Jacquard's loom, the weaver would place each warp thread by hand, a very time-consuming and error-prone process. Jacquard's loom allowed a single operator to weave intricate patterns with very little handwork.

Smithsonian Institution negative #77042

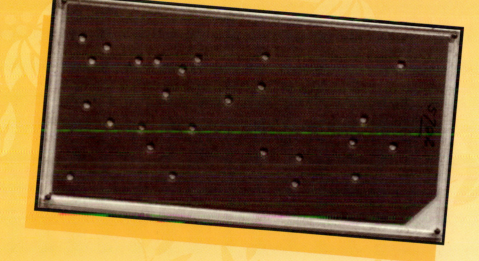

Some Punched Cards   In Jacquard's loom, each warp thread hangs from a metal rod with a hook on the end. Each rod in turn is controlled by a particular hole in a punched card. If the card has a hole, then that rod (and its corresponding thread) is allowed to cross the loom. A series of cards, tied together to form a loop, creates a repeating pattern. Punched cards used in the twentieth century, such as the UNIVAC card shown at bottom, are based on the Jacquard mechanism.

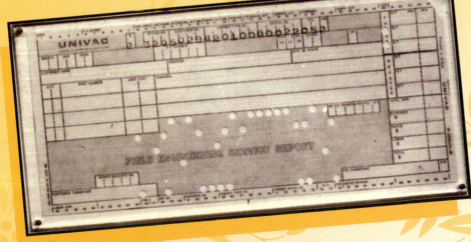

Smithsonian Institution negative #77034

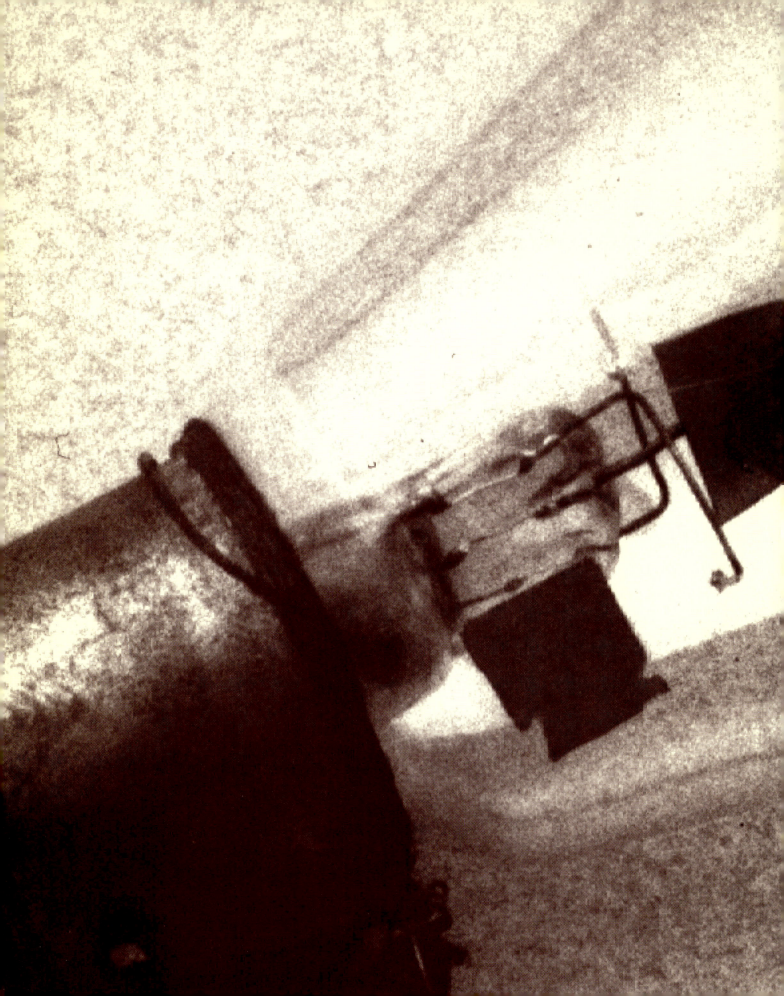

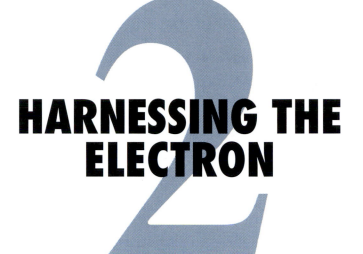

HARNESSING THE ELECTRON

CONTENTS

THE EARLY CALCULATOR builders, and Babbage in particular, were often frustrated by the limitations of the technology of their day. It was a technology of brass and steel, springs and gears—quite similar in many ways to the technology of mechanical watchmaking.

While working on some astronomic tables, the young Babbage once exclaimed to a friend, "I wish to God that these calculations had been executed by steam." Ironically, had Babbage succeeded in building his full-sized Analytical Engine, he would have needed a steam engine to produce enough power to turn the hundreds of gears and cams inside the machine. While steam provided a reliable source of power for everything from automobiles to locomotives, it was not the ideal power source for number crunching.

Even though electricity had been discovered over a century before Babbage's time, it remained more of a laboratory curiosity than a practical tool during his lifetime. In 1879, eight years after Babbage's death, Thomas Edison (1847–1931) perfected the light bulb. This single invention moved electricity out of the laboratory and into virtually every home and business. Although Edison himself was not concerned with computers, his many inventions had a direct and profound effect on the shape of things to come.

Edison was a staunch proponent of and one of the first suppliers of commercial electric power. His goal was to replace all forms of lighting (candles, oil lamps, and so on) with safer and cheaper electric power. Of course, Edison also intended to provide the light bulbs, wiring, switches, and even the power itself, thus earning him a great fortune. Two of his companies—Edison Power and General Electric—survive to this day. Edison's success and the wide availability of commercial electricity prompted thousands of inventors to find new ways to harness the power of the electron.

In particular, Edison's invention of the light bulb led to the discovery of the vacuum tube, a building block of the early computer systems. Edison himself had noted the odd emissions from the filaments of his light bulbs, but he was too busy with other projects to pursue the commercial value of those emissions. However, several years later, English physicist Sir John Ambrose Fleming took the time to investigate those emissions, which came to be known as the *Edison Effect*. Fleming's observations led to his creation of the first vacuum tube. American inventor Lee DeForest improved on Fleming's design, and DeForest's Audion tube became the foundation of the broadcasting industry.

Electricity and the vacuum tube were the "enabling technologies" for the first generation of digital computers, and it is doubtful that we would have any computers today were it not for electric power. But it took the second World War to prompt computer scientists to discover ways to overcome many new and almost insurmountable challenges of that era.

CHAPTER
3

Punched Cards and the Birth of IBM

NEARLY A HUNDRED years passed between the invention of Jacquard's loom and the subjects of this chapter. During that time, the Industrial Revolution crossed the Atlantic, spreading from England to France to post-Civil War America. As in Europe, the American Industrial Revolution caused a major population shift when farm workers moved to the city to fill new jobs in manufacturing. The railroad (itself a product of the Industrial Revolution) made cross-country travel possible, effectively moving San Francisco many weeks closer to New York. Morse had developed the telegraph and Edison invented the electric light bulb. Business was booming and America became a land of opportunity.

In response to promise of opportunity, hundreds of thousands of immigrants came to America, many of whom were skilled workers. The wave of immigration also brought some of the brightest minds from Europe to America, including many scientists and inventors. But no change is without problems, and the sudden influx of people put a tremendous burden on the Census Bureau.

Seven years into the tallying the 1880 census, the bureau realized that they would not finish counting the 1890 census before it was time to begin the 1900 census. The bureau took a novel approach to their problem: They held a competition to find a better way to collect, count, and sort the census data. After three finalists were chosen, another contest was devised to select a winner. They would perform a small sample census of St. Louis, Missouri. Herman Hollerith (1860–1929), American-born son of German immigrant parents, won easily, besting his nearest opponent by a time of $5\frac{1}{2}$ hours to 44 hours.

Like Babbage before him, Hollerith reached back into Jean-Marie Jacquard's bag of tricks. Specifically, he devised a system to collect the census data on punched paper cards. Holes in the cards represented the number of persons in the household, the family's ethnic background, literacy level, occupations, and other data. The census taker punched out the appropriate holes on a card for each family, and the cards were placed into a machine called a card reader. This machine used an electric current to sense the presence or absence of holes in each part of the card. As each card was inserted into the card reader, the machine added the data on the card to the previous totals held in the machine. The result was displayed on numeric dials on the front of the machine.

It is important to note that Hollerith's machine did not actually perform any computation or analysis on the data; it simply kept a running total of the data fed into it via the punched cards. Each day's batch of cards had to be manually added to the prior day's batch in order to keep a running total. Still, it was a vast improvement over the prior system of manually entering the data into ledger pads!

Hollerith won the support of the census bureau, and they hired him to supervise the collection of data for the 1890 census. Mr. Hollerith thus became the world's first data processing manager. The 1890 census was a success, requiring only six weeks to complete. Hollerith and his machine were much in demand, and in 1896 he formed the Tabulating Machine Company to sell his products and services to the business world.

In 1911, the Tabulating Machine Company merged with two other companies. International Time Recording Company made mechanical time clocks, and the Computing Scale Company made a computing scale used by merchants. Together, the three companies became the Computing-Tabulating-Recording Company, or C-T-R. In 1924, the company changed its name to International Business Machines; we know it today as IBM.

Incidentally (and perhaps prophetically) Hollerith's punched cards were the exact size of the old dollar bill. Sixty years later, IBM's gross income (for fiscal year 1983) was $40 billion, more than the gross national product of many countries.

Hollerith's Card Reader

Back before we had PCs on every desk, the punched card was as close as most people got to a computer. The first commercial use of punched cards was in the 1890 census, when Herman Hollerith's punched-card-based counting system tallied the entire United States population in six weeks—a job that had previously taken seven years.

An Early Card Reader (1888) This machine, looking a bit like a cross between an upright piano and a pants press, is the original Hollerith card reader used in the 1890 census. To use the machine, the operator placed a card in the reader (on the right side of the desktop) and pulled the handle. This lowered a group of spring-loaded wires onto the surface of the card. If the card had a hole in a given position, the wire would pass through the card and into a small cup of mercury below the reader. When the wire touched the mercury, it completed an electrical circuit, moving the count incrementally on the dial assigned to that particular hole.

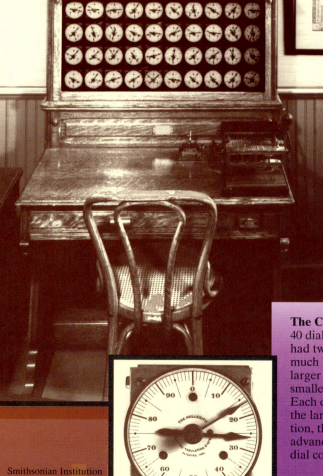

Smithsonian Institution negative # 79-10952

Smithsonian Institution negative # 64555

The Counting Dials Each of the 40 dials on the face of the machine had two hands. The hands worked much like clock hands, with the larger hand indicating units and the smaller indicating hundreds of units. Each dial had 100 positions; once the large hand completed a revolution, the smaller "hundreds" hand advanced to the next position. Each dial could could count up to 10,000.

Courtesy of IBM

An Automatic Card Reader (1930s)   This machine was one of the first completely automatic card readers. Instead of the one-at-a-time operation of the earlier machines, this reader could process an entire stack of cards. A motor-driven mechanism pulled a card from the bottom of the incoming stack into the reader head, where electrical contacts read the card. The card was then ejected and stashed at the bottom of another stack This design was refined several times over the next 50 years, and modern-day card readers can read hundreds of cards per minute.

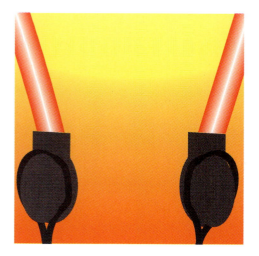

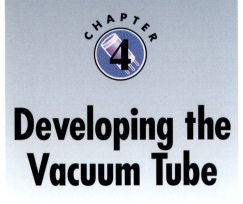

Developing the Vacuum Tube

I F YOU READ many computer magazines, you've probably heard the term "enabling technology." This term is used to define a basic technological breakthrough that makes subsequent progress possible. For the earliest electronic computers, the enabling technology was the vacuum tube.

The machines we've seen so far have one thing in common: They are all mechanical devices. Babbage had planned to power his massive differential engine with steam, but the actual computing work would have been done with gears and cams. Several other inventors, notably Lord Kelvin (1842–1907), built analytical computers after Babbage, but theirs were also mechanical devices. The inner workings of the readout dials on Hollerith's card reader were still mechanical, even though the machine was powered by electricity and used electric current to sense the presence of holes in the cards.

Commercial electric power first became available in the 1890s. By the turn of the century, humankind had developed only a very basic repertoire of electrical talents that specifically included motors and electric lighting. Light bulbs were expensive and fragile, and many inventors set out to find a better way to make them. One of these inventors was none other than Thomas Edison.

In 1883, Edison noticed that a current would flow in one direction from the filament of a light bulb to a metal plate inside the bulb. Since this discovery didn't apply directly to the performance or longevity of the light bulb, Edison simply made a note of the phenomenon (modestly naming it the Edison Effect), and continued with his work.

The Edison Effect went virtually unnoticed until 1904 when English inventor John Ambrose Fleming (1849–1945), a former Edison employee, went to work for the Marconi Radio Company office in London as chief scientific advisor. Fleming's first assignment was to develop a more sensitive radio signal detector. This improvement would enable long distance radio communications using much lower-powered transmitters than the ones that were practical at the time. Fleming recalled Edison's observation of the Edison Effect and decided to try to adapt the light bulb for use as a radio wave detector.

Fleming soon discovered that the Edison Effect did not work in reverse. Further, Fleming discovered that radio waves passed into the tube could be converted to a varying direct current, which could in turn be passed into earphones, thus re-creating the original sound. Fleming named his tube the oscillation valve, and filed for a patent.

Unfortunately for Fleming, another team at Marconi was pursuing a different type of radio wave detector—the galena crystal detector. The galena crystal detector worked nearly as well as Fleming's oscillation valve, and was cheaper and easier to produce. This development cause the Marconi Company to shelve Fleming's valve and build their receivers around a galena crystal detector.

Back across the Atlantic, radio pioneer Lee DeForest (1873–1961) was also working to develop a better radio detector circuit. DeForest read about Fleming's valve and decided to build one for himself. In 1906, he added a third element, the grid, to the Fleming tube. The grid consists of a zigzag piece of nickel wire placed between the tube's filament and the plate. Electrons normally flow from the filament to the plate, but even a small charge applied to the grid interrupts the flow of electrons. Thus, by applying a weak signal (like a radio wave) to the plate, a stronger, amplified signal is created at the plate. The amplified signal is identical to the grid signal but is much stronger. The addition of the grid resulted in the creation of the vacuum tube as we know it today.

DeForest's tube, called the Audion (we know it today as the triode), was exactly the right invention at the right time. Besides providing a better radio wave detector, the vacuum tube provided enough amplification to allow the use of loudspeakers. For the first time, people could listen to the radio without being burdened by headphones.

Ironically, it appears that DeForest himself did not understand how his invention worked because like Edison, he was much more a pragmatist than a scientist. In a patent application, DeForest confessed that he was unable to explain how the Audion functioned as an amplifier of electrical signals. All that mattered was that it worked, and work it did. DeForest's mysterious invention laid the foundation for the entire electronics industry and provided an essential building block for radio, television, and the first electronic computers.

The Vacuum Tube

Initially discovered by Thomas Edison in 1883, the vacuum tube formed the building block for the entire electronics industry. Because Edison was trying at the time to create a better light bulb, he didn't pay much attention to the potential value of the tube within the bulb.

The Edison Effect (1883)   During his quest for a better light bulb, Edison—an indefatigable tinkerer—tried hundreds of combinations of filament materials and configurations. At one point, he added an extra metal plate inside the bulb, hoping that the plate would collect the black soot given off by the carbon filament. Although the plate didn't help the soot problem, Edison noticed that a current applied to the filament could flow through the vacuum to the plate. Edison didn't know it at the time, but he had invented the *diode*—a one-way valve for electric current. Because it didn't solve his immediate problem—the soot inside the bulb—Edison made a note of the phenomenon, naming it the Edison Effect. He noted that the phenomenon might one day be used to measure electric currents, and he even filed for a patent on such a device. This was one of the few times Edison didn't realize what he had.

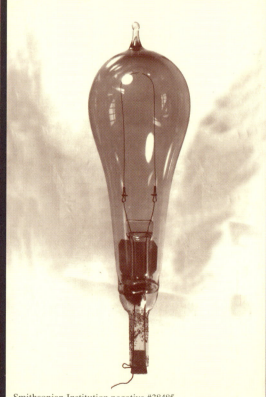

Smithsonian Institution negative #38485

An Edison Light Bulb (1884)   Edison's original electric bulb was quite similar to the ones we use today. It consisted of a carbon filament (modern bulbs use tungsten wire) enclosed in a vacuum inside a glass bulb. An electric current flowing through the filament causes the filament to heat up and glow. Since there is no oxygen inside the vacuum, the filament does not burn up but continues to glow as long as power is applied. However, the filament eventually breaks down from the repeated stress of heating up and cooling off.

| 1875 | 1880 | **1884** | 1885 | 1890 |

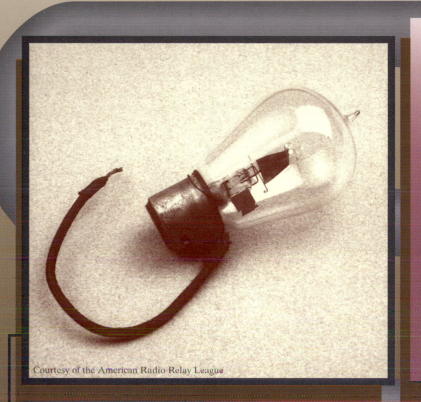

Courtesy of the American Radio Relay League

Fleming's Valve (1904) A few years after Edison's observation of the Edison Effect, former Edison researcher John Ambrose Fleming attempted to adapt the Edison valve for use as a radio wave detector. Fleming made a discovery even more remarkable than Edison's. He discovered that the alternating current of a radio signal, when applied to the filament of the tube, could be converted into a varying direct current. Fleming now truly understood the one-way nature of the tube, and he coined the phrase *electric valve* to describe the operation of the tube. Fleming's employer, the Marconi Radio Company office in London, showed little interest in his invention, having discovered a better, cheaper way to convert radio waves to direct current. The patent for this invention was issued in 1904.

DeForest's Audion Tube (1906) Around the same time as Fleming's discovery, inventor Lee DeForest was also searching for a better way to detect radio waves. Hearing of Fleming's work from a scientific journal, DeForest—a tinkerer in the Edison School—built his own vacuum tube. But DeForest's tube was different in that it had a third element, a grid, positioned between the plate and the filament. DeForest discovered that a current placed on the grid could control the flow of electrons from the filament to the plate, thus creating an amplified version of the signal applied to the grid. DeForest had built the first signal amplifier, and his discovery allowed the construction of vastly improved radio sets and transmitters.

Smithsonian Institution negative #64934

Heavy Metal Dinosaurs

NO, THIS CHAPTER isn't about Led Zeppelin, Aerosmith, or Spinal Tap. It's about computers—the first true computers that are being covered in this book: Kelvin's tide predictor, the MIT differential analyzer, and the Harvard Mark I. These are computers from the Jurassic era of computing—a period when the fundamental concepts of computing were just beginning to be understood. As you'll see, the computers from this era were technological dinosaurs—many were obsolete before they were completed. Like the dinosaurs, these computers became extinct. Nevertheless they had a profound impact on the development of the next generation of computers.

Today, all the information our computers can process—words, numbers, and pictures—is represented by a series of binary 1s and 0s. This is why virtually all modern-day computers are digital systems, which means they internally use the binary system of mathematical notation. But one of the first true computing machines was neither binary nor digital, yet it performed a very important function.

In the early 1870s, the great Scottish physicist William Thomson (Lord Kelvin) was asked to devise a machine to predict the tide for any given date. Tidal computations are quite complex; the tide is affected by both Earth's position relative to the sun, and the moon's position relative to Earth. To compute the tide for a given time on a given day in a given location, you must first compute the position of Earth in relation to the sun and moon. Mathematically, the problem of tide computation can be represented by a pair of differential equations; one to compute the sun's effect, and another to compute the moon's pull.

All of this tidal theory was well understood in Kelvin's time, and Kelvin set out to build a tide predictor machine. With the help of his brother, James Thomson, Kelvin completed the machine in 1876. It worked remarkably well, and became standard-issue equipment for all major English seaports. Kelvin's machine was essentially a computer, although it was analog, not digital, in operation.

While working on the tide predictor, Kelvin realized that the basic idea behind the tide predictor could be applied to any mathematical problem. In a paper published by the Royal Society in 1876, Kelvin suggested the idea of a "differential analyzer" that would, like his tide computer, be capable of solving multiple differential equations. But the differential analyzer would be distinguished by its ability to solve *any* differential equation, not just those concerning the positions of the sun and moon. Like Babbage's earlier proposal for the Difference Engine, the machine would be enormous and entirely mechanical, perhaps driven by electric motors. Unlike Babbage, Lord Kelvin was quite busy with other endeavors, and he didn't attempt to build the beast.

Kelvin's idea sat idle for nearly 50 years. In 1930, Vennevar Bush, a professor at the Massachusetts Institute of Technology (MIT), built a machine remarkably like Kelvin had proposed. Bush even borrowed the name *differential analyzer* when referring to his machine. He claimed not to have read Kelvin's paper until some time after the MIT analyzer was completed, but the two machines are strikingly similar in concept.

Bush's analyzer was a mechanical-electronic hybrid because he realized that an all-mechanical machine would be truly enormous. That's where vacuum tubes came to the rescue. Bush used the tubes as a temporary storage medium, roughly equivalent to the random access memory (RAM) of today's computers. Bush's use of vacuum tubes was a first, although the machine still grew to be over 50 feet long. Nevertheless, the machine worked reliably, and several copies were built.

From a technical standpoint, the MIT analyzer was a dead-end technology. Although it was at least partially electronic, it still used mostly mechanical components. Nevertheless, it was a significant accomplishment for its time, and it represented the first of a short-lived generation of tube-based computers.

The next step in computer science, the Harvard Mark I, was both a step forward and a step backward. This machine (also known as the IBM Mark I) was built in 1943 by a team of scientists at Harvard University, with funding provided by IBM. The Mark I was electromechanical, not electronic. Howard Aiken, its principal designer, dismissed vacuum tubes as being too inefficient and unreliable. Instead of using tubes, Aiken built the Mark I with thousands of electromechanical relays, which are essentially electrically operated switches. They use a current flowing in one circuit to open or close a switch in another circuit. When compared to the modern-day transistor (see Chapter 8), relays are slow, taking a few hundred milliseconds to perform an operation. This inherent slowness carried through the entire design of the Mark I, where the action of one relay might affect dozens or even hundreds of others in the machine. Also, relays produce a loud noise when they open or close—the Mark I was very noisy. Finally, relays are relatively large, and the completed Mark I was 8 feet tall and, like Bush's analyzer, it was also over 50 feet long! IBM president Thomas Watson insisted that the machine be covered with a streamlined glass and stainless steel case to make the machine look more futuristic. The completed machine contained nearly a million parts and weighed several tons.

Internally, the Mark I was basically an electromechanical re-creation of Babbage's Analytical Engine. Both of these machines used decimal notation, unlike today's binary machines. The Mark I could perform calculations up to 23 digits long. It could also compute three additions per second, but took 6 seconds to perform a multiplication and 12 seconds to divide two numbers. However, the Mark I was much faster than any previous computer (although a much faster machine soon came along shortly after it).

The U.S. Navy pressed the Mark I into service during World War II. After the war, the machine received an enormous amount of publicity, with its Art-Deco facade appearing in *Life*, *Look*, and the *Saturday Evening Post*. The Mark I wasn't the most important computer of the war era (more about those machines in the next chapter), but it was the best known at the time.

The Mark I's biggest contribution to the world of computing was simple: It placed IBM in the public's eye, launching it to the forefront of the fledgling computing industry. People who didn't know anything else about computers at least knew those three letters: IBM.

The First True Computers

These three machines, though quite varied in design and operation, were among the first successful computing machines. Each broke new ground in a specific area of computer science, and all modern-day computers owe part of their design to these machines.

The Science Museum/Science and Society Picture Library

Kelvin's Tide Predictor (1876)
This machine could predict the high and low tide times for any date in the future. To use the machine, the operator entered past tidal observation data using the ten wheels at the top of the machine. Turning the crank operated the machine's computational engine, and the resulting tide table was printed out as a paper graph on the front of the machine. This may be the first use of computer-generated graphical output—sort of a Victorian-era Macintosh.

1870   **1876**   1880   1890   1900   1910

Courtesy of the MIT Museum

The MIT Differential Analyzer (1930)
This room-sized machine was built in
1930 by MIT mathematician Vannevar
Bush. The basic computational engine
was mechanical, but the machine used
vacuum tubes (then a relatively new
technology) for temporary storage.
The machine could only solve differential equations, so it was not a general-purpose computer in the true
sense of the term. The machine's program was determined by the position
of gears on shafts. To program the machine for a specific calucation, the
shafts and gears had to be carefully rearranged—a time-consuming process.

Courtesy of IBM Archives

The IBM/Harvard Mark I (1943)   The Mark I was the first completely automatic, digital com-
puter. It was essentially an electomechanical re-creation of Babbage's Analytical Engine. The
Mark I was pressed into service performing naval weapons calculations during World War II.
The Mark I was even larger and more impressive than the MIT analyzer; it was 55 feet long,
8 feet high, and 3½ feet deep. It weighed several tons and had nearly a million components.
Originally named the Automatic Sequence Controlled Calculator, the Mark I was designed by
Harvard professor Howard Aiken and built at IBM's Endicott, New York factory. The com-
pleted machine was then disassembled and shipped to Harvard, where the Mark I remained in
service for 15 years.

1920   **1930**   1940 **1943**   1950   1960

What World War II Did for Technology

I T IS AN unfortunate truth that much technological innovation is born in wartime. This was especially the case with the second World War, perhaps the first war won almost entirely by technology. At least part of the Allied success against the Nazis must be attributed to the fact that the Allies could intercept and read virtually every Nazi dispatch. The Nazis believed that their document encryption system was entirely secure when in reality, the English were reading their most secret and sensitive mail.

Prior to the start of World War II, the German Navy developed a cipher machine named Enigma. The Enigma machine could automatically encode a message in such a way that only another Enigma machine could decode it. In order to read a ciphered message, the operator of the receiving Enigma machine would enter a special code called a key into the machine. The key codes were changed frequently—sometimes hourly—and were hand-delivered by courier to prevent them from falling into the wrong hands. The United States, England, and Japan all had similar cipher systems.

In 1938, the Polish Secret Service managed to steal an Enigma machine and smuggle it to England. English cryptoanalysts studied the machine to learn how it worked, and devised a method to crack the Enigma code. Unfortunately, code-cracking is very complex work, and it took hours to decode even the simplest of messages by hand. In 1939, the British Secret Service assigned a team of mathematicians and scientists to tackle the problem. The project was code-named Ultra, and was housed in an old country mansion in Bletchley, 50 miles north of London.

The project Ultra team devised a series of code-cracking computers, beginning with a Mark I-like machine built with electromechanical relays, and culminating with a machine called the Colossus. The Colossus was entirely electronic, the mechanical relays of earlier designs having been replaced with much faster vacuum tubes. The Colossus machine could digest Enigma-ciphered information at the rate of about 5,000 characters per second, a remarkable rate even by today's standards. At the peak of the war, ten Colossus machines operated night and day, deciphering as many as 2,000 messages per day. The deciphered messages were hand-carried back to London for use by the British high command.

The Nazis, confident that the Enigma cipher system was uncrackable, used the system throughout the war. Because of the assumed level of secrecy, virtually every important Nazi command—even those from Hitler himself—was transmitted via Enigma-ciphered radio transmissions. Meanwhile, the Allies could read every word of every "secret" Nazi dispatch. The English actually had to be very careful how they used the intercepted information; any obvious defensive move might tip off the Nazis. English Prime Minister Sir Winston Churchill is reported to have allowed several Nazi bombing raids to go unopposed; to do otherwise would have revealed that the English had broken the Enigma code.

Designed specifically to crack the Enigma code, the Colossus wasn't a general-purpose machine like the Mark I, but it was the world's first entirely electronic digital computer. It proved that an electronic machine could handle mind-numbing amounts of data, and it also proved that an all-electronic computer could run circles around IBM's relay-driven Mark I.

Ironically, the Nazis nearly had similar computer technology in their own hands, but they let it slip away. In 1936, a German engineering student named Konrad Zuse set out to build a binary digital computer system. Working in his parents' home, Zuse built a working electromechanical computer from erector-set parts. He named the machine the Z1, and it may have been the first binary computer ever built. Zuse's computer had a keyboard for input and a series of light bulbs to display the computer's output. Satisfied that his basic design was sound, Zuse built a second machine, the Z2. The Z2 used electromechanical relays much like those of the IBM Mark I, and it used a punched tape system for input and output much like later computers used.

Zuse contemplated building a vacuum-tube–based machine, but tubes in wartime Germany were virtually impossible to get. Hoping to get government backing for his work, Zuse approached the German government about the possibility of building a high-speed computer to help crack enemy ciphered messages. The Nazi authorities didn't see any value in Zuse's machine and sent him on his way.

During the closing months of the war, Zuse fled to southern Germany. After the war, he began work on one of the first computer languages, and started a computer company of his own. His company, Zuse AG, was acquired by the German computer giant Siemens in 1969.

Had the Germans seen the value in Zuse's machine, the war may have turned out quite differently. The Nazis had tried without success to crack the English and American code machines. Having high-speed computer technology would have given the Nazis the ability to break the Allied codes as well as the ability to create a more so-phisticated cipher system than the Enigma could offer. Further, at the end of the war, the German nuclear weapons program was only a year or two away from producing a working nuclear weapon. A high-speed computer like the one Zuse had proposed may have given the Nazis a large step towards completion of a nuclear bomb.

Across the Atlantic, American computer engineers were also quite busy during the war. The U.S. military faced a maddening problem that concerned trajectory tables. A *trajectory table* is an important document that is required for every new model of gun or missile. As a projectile travels away from a gun, the forces of air friction and gravity combine, causing the projectile to fall in an arc until it eventually hits the ground. A trajectory table tells the gunner how far the projectile will fall on its way to the target, so the gunner knows how high to tilt the gun barrel to hit a target at a given distance. As you might guess, the calculation of these tables was tedious and time-consuming, and they had to be very accurate. Engineers could design and build new and more ef-fective weapons, but those weapons couldn't be used until all the paperwork—the tra-jectory table—was complete.

In 1942, the U.S. Army Ordinance Corps commissioned a team of scientists at the University of Pennsylvania's Moore School of Electrical Engineering to design a top-secret electronic machine that could compute trajectory tables quickly. The leader of the team was Dr. John Mauchly; his chief assistant was a 22-year-old engineer named J. Presper Eckert. Mauchly and Eckert had never built a computer before, but they were very familiar with the work of Bush, Aiken, and Babbage. From the start, Mauchly and Eckert decided that if their machine was to be as fast as possible, it would have to be an all-electronic machine, using vacuum-tube technology. What they didn't know at the outset was that their machine would use 18,000 of the tubes. They also didn't know about the Colossus project, which only required about 2,400 tubes, because Colossus was still wrapped in a shroud of secrecy.

Working around the clock for 30 months, they finally finished their machine, the Electronic Numerical Integrator And Calculator (ENIAC for short), in February of 1946—just before the end of the war. At the time, ENIAC was the largest and most complex electronic device ever built. It was also heralded for many years as being the first all-electronic computer, even though Colossus beat it by three years (the British government kept Colossus an official state secret until 1974).

The completed ENIAC weighed 60,000 pounds, occupied 1,500 square feet of floor space, and required a staff of 5 operators to keep it running. It also required enormous amounts of ventilation to remove the heat generated by the vacuum tubes—and it consumed prodigious amounts of power as well. Legend has it that the lights of Philadelphia dimmed noticeably every time ENIAC was switched on.

Despite the fact that it was completed too late to fulfill its original mission, ENIAC remained in service for 10 years, computing gun, bomb, and missile trajectory tables for the armed forces. Contrary to popular myth, ENIAC was not used in the U.S. nuclear weapons (Manhattan) project, although Manhattan project engineer John Von Neumann worked with the Moore team on their next project—which I'll get to in a moment.

ENIAC was very much the prototype for all modern computers, except in one very important area. Like every computer before it, ENIAC's one and only program was designed into the computer itself. Although it was possible to alter ENIAC's internal program, doing so required an extensive amount of rewiring, often taking several days.

After the war, Mauchly and Eckert, with the help of Von Neumann, assessed what they had accomplished with ENIAC. They realized that ENIAC's weakest point was that it could only store and run one program at a time. This conclusion caused them to build a new machine to correct this shortcoming, and eventually they started a company to build the new computer. As we'll see in Part 3 of this book, their next project would launch an entire industry.

Cracking the Code

The second World War accelerated computing research like no event before or since. Perhaps the most amazing story of wartime computing is the English effort to build a cipher-busting computer called the Colossus. In 1936, a Polish mechanic employed in the Enigma factory smuggled a set of Enigma plans to the Allies. Later that year, a Polish Secret Service agent managed to get hold of an entire Enigma machine, which was promptly smuggled into England. English cryptoanalysts devised a way to crack the Enigma code. The English Secret Service set up a covert think-tank operation, code-named Ultra, to build code-cracking machines. The resulting machine was Colossus, the first all-electronic digital computer. Ten Colossus machines were built, each using about 2,400 vacuum tubes. The machines ran night and day for the duration of the war in Europe, deciphering as many as 2,000 Enigma messages each day.

| 1931 | 1932 | 1933 | 1934 | 1935 |

Smithsonian Institution
negative #90-3649

**The Enigma Machine
(1939)**   This machine, looking
somewhat like a typewriter in
a box, caused the Allies no
small amount of grief. This is
the Enigma cipher machine,
devised by the German navy
just prior to the outbreak of
hostilities in 1939. Ironically,
the design of the Enigma machine was based partially on
earlier United States-made
cipher machines.

Messages that were Enigma
ciphered were mixed with a
random word or phrase called
a key. Once ciphered, the resulting message looked like
gibberish until it was fed into
another Enigma machine and
decoded with the proper key.
The Nazis believed the Enigma
system to be uncrackable, and
they used the machine for virtually every sensitive document and order. The ciphered
Enigma messages were usually
transmitted via short-wave
radio, making them easy to
receive in nearby England.

ENIAC

Brute Force Computing This is the ENIAC, the first U.S.-built all-electronic computer. It was completed in 1946. As you can see, ENIAC was a monster, occupying 1,500 square feet of floor space to house more than 18,000 vacuum tubes. In operation, ENIAC drew so much power that according to legend, the lights of Philadelphia dimmed when the machine was switched on. Those 18,000 tubes generated an enormous amount of heat, and a special ventilation system was built to keep cool air flowing over the machine.

Programming ENIAC ENIAC was a fixed-program computer, designed specifically to perform ballistics calculations. Before each set of calculations was run, operators entered the raw data into ENIAC using telephone-operator–style plugs. Once programmed and running, ENIAC could perform 5,000 additions or 300 multiplications per second—about 1,000 times the speed of the IBM Mark I.

1930   1940   (**1946**)   1950

Smithsonian Institution
negative #53192

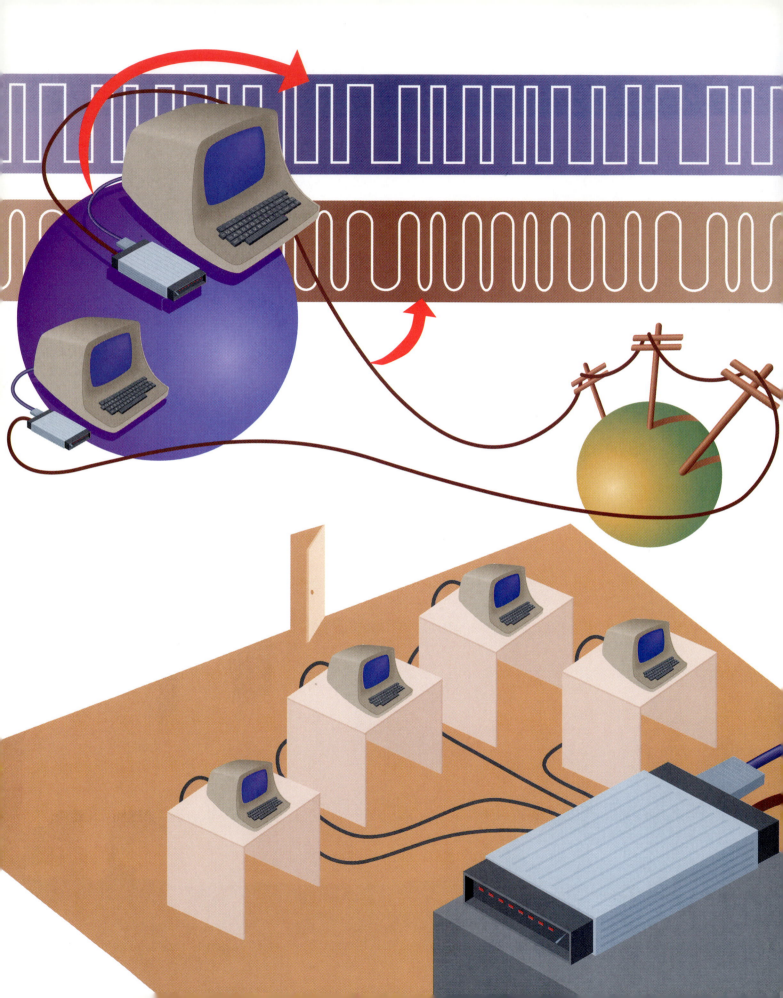

BUILDING AN INDUSTRY

CONTENTS

EACH OF THE machines we've seen so far—ENIAC, Mark I, and Colossus—represented a very large step toward our modern concept of computing. Each was designed with a single purpose in mind, and each was almost completely inflexible in that design. Those machines ran a single program—a program that was often built into the machine itself. Despite their single-mindedness, those early machines served their intended purposes quite well, accomplishing tasks that otherwise might not have been possible.

The next step forward in computing was the creation of machines that could run a variety of programs. These programmable machines were much more flexible and more useful than their predecessors. In fact, they were so flexible that they could be adapted to suit virtually any task that required data collection and computation. This flexibility did not go unnoticed in the business community.

If the ENIAC, Mark I, and Colossus represented the birth of the electronic computer, then the EDVAC, UNIVAC, and IBM 650 represented the birth of the computer industry. When IBM introduced the model 650 computer in 1956, they estimated the total demand for the machine at 50 to 60 units. Several years later, there were several thousand IBM 650s humming away at mundane tasks like accounting, bill collecting, and census-taking. By 1984, IBM was the largest manufacturing company in the world—and the largest company that had ever existed.

For many people, the three letters *IBM* were synonymous with *computer*, not unlike calling a photocopier a Xerox machine. This was certainly no accident, but a result of two factors. First, there was IBM's relentless sales force, led by the legendary Thomas J. Watson. IBM may not have always had the best products, but they always had the best salespeople. The second factor was IBM's blank-check research and development program, rivaled only by AT&T's Bell Labs. IBM routinely hired the best and brightest computer engineers, physicists, chemists, and other scientists, and gave them huge amounts of funding for basic research. That research paid off many times for IBM, resulting in numerous important technological innovations.

Ironically, it was a Bell Labs invention that set the entire electronics industry on its ear, and that provided IBM with the essential building block of the modern computer. That invention was the *transistor*—a simple chunk of melted sand with a few wires stuck into it. The transistor could do everything a vacuum tube could do, but it was far faster and more rugged, reliable, and efficient.

As computers became smaller, faster, and more reliable, they also came down in price—a trend that continues to this day. Once the province of large universities and research labs, the computer became an essential business tool.

Computers Go to Work

I N 1944, BEFORE THE ENIAC was even completed, mathematician John Von Neumann joined up with ENIAC developers John Mauchly and Presper Eckert to plan an improved version of the ENIAC. They began by assessing the weak and strong points of ENIAC. ENIAC's strong point was its speed. The use of vacuum tubes had been a brilliant choice, and ENIAC performed as well as expected despite the frequent failure of the fragile tubes. Since there was little that could be done about ENIAC's weak point—the reliability of the tubes—the team focused their energies on the operational aspects of ENIAC.

While ENIAC had been a success, the machine itself was quite difficult to operate. Reprogramming ENIAC required a team of technicians who essentially rewired the machine to change its single built-in program. As a result, ENIAC spent much of its time sitting idle while program changes were made.

There had to be a better way, and Von Neumann suggested that the next machine should store its program within the computer itself. This was a radical step and a brilliant move: The stored-program concept changed the entire face of computing. Instead of sitting idle for days at a time, the computer could switch programs by itself in a matter of seconds. The tedious switch-flipping and plug-cord patching of ENIAC would become a thing of the past. Once written, a program could be stored on punched paper tape and reused indefinitely. A program could even load other programs through a process called *chaining*.

The trio of Mauchly, Eckert, and Von Neumann set out to build their new machine, the Electronic Discrete Variable Automatic Computer, or EDVAC. Eckert and Mauchly left the Moore School before EDVAC was finished, and together they formed the Eckert-Mauchly Computer Corporation. Without their leadership, the EDVAC project fell behind schedule, and the recognition of developing the first working stored-program computer fell to Professor Maurice Wilkes at Cambridge University in England. Wilkes had attended lectures by Mauchly and Eckert at the Moore School, and he obviously didn't sleep through the lectures. Wilkes's computer was completed in May of 1949, nearly two years before EDVAC.

At their newly formed company, Eckert and Mauchly began work on an even more powerful machine, the Universal Automatic Calculator, or UNIVAC. In 1950, the Eckert-Mauchly Computer

Corporation was acquired by Remington-Rand Corporation. The first Remington UNIVAC-1 was delivered to the U.S. Census Bureau in 1951, where it remained in service for 12 years. Upon its retirement in 1963, it was moved to the Smithsonian Institution in Washington—to right next to the ENIAC. The next four UNIVACs also went into service in government agencies in the Army, Air Force, Navy, and Atomic Energy Commission.

The first UNIVAC sold to a private company was purchased by General Electric Corporation, thus becoming the first computer acquired by a private business. There is some irony in GE's purchase of a UNIVAC. General Electric is the successor company to Thomas Edison's original Edison Electric Company. Edison, you will remember, had first noted the Edison Effect, the precursor to the vacuum tube. GE was one of the world's largest manufacturers of vacuum tubes, yet the company was not at all involved in applying that technology to the task of computation. GE later made a halfhearted attempt to enter the computer business—along with dozens of other companies. By the time GE entered the race, IBM, Sperry, and several other companies were already well established.

Where was IBM while all these UNIVACs were being sold? As of 1950, IBM chairman Thomas Watson, Sr., wasn't sure that the company should get too deeply involved in the computer business. IBM was already making plenty of money by supplying punched card equipment, typewriters, time clocks, and other office equipment to the business world. Most of IBM's products—like the Mark I computer—were electro-mechanical, not electronic, devices. One IBM executive described the engineering staff as "Edisonian," an apt description. They were quite comfortable working with Edison-era technology like relays, wires, and motors, but they were out of their league working with the digital technology of computers. Entering the computer business would require a substantial investment in basic research and development, manufacturing facilities, and personnel. Besides, the senior Watson argued, IBM's existing customers seemed to be getting along fine with the company's current offerings, and there was no guarantee that there really was much of a market for computers. Watson's fears were shared by the rest of the industry. John Mauchly had at one time estimated that there were perhaps twelve organizations in the world that both needed and could afford a UNIVAC. Nevertheless, Remington eventually sold forty UNIVAC systems.

In the end, it was Thomas Watson, Jr., who made the decision to go ahead with IBM's electronic computer project. Given the benefit of 20/20 hindsight, we all know that he made the right choice. At the time, however, it was a risky move—one that could have bankrupted the company had it gone wrong.

Watson called the project the Defense Calculator. The name implied that the project was being done for the government market, and it was chosen to ease some of the opposition inside IBM. By the time the machine was ready for delivery in 1952, it had been renamed the IBM 701.

IBM hired a team of bright young engineers, many of them straight out of college, to design and build the 701. Because most of them had no previous exposure to computers, they were free of any preconceived ideas about what a computer should be.

The first IBM 701 was delivered early in 1953. The 701 was a landmark computer in many ways. In some respects it was not as powerful as the UNIVAC-1, but in many ways it was much more powerful and flexible. The 701 was built in several separate units, which allowed IBM to build the machine and ship it, complete, to the customer's computer room. The UNIVAC, being one large unit, had to be assembled at the customer's site, and could not easily be moved once installed. Perhaps the most significant technological innovation in the 701 was the use of magnetic plastic tape as a storage medium—the first computer to do so.

Initially marketed as a scientific computer, the 701 soon found its way into general-purpose data processing applications. In fact, it was an IBM executive, James Birkenstock, who coined the term *Electronic Data Processing*—a term now used to define the entire computer industry. The 701 was a smashing success, exceeding all sales expectations.

Before the first 701 was delivered, another group within IBM proposed to build a smaller, cheaper computer—the model 650—aimed at the still-undefined "general purpose" computing market. The decision to build the 650 prompted an even more heated debate than had the 701. IBM's all-powerful Sales and Product Planning group said that it would not be able to sell any 650s because the machine would be too expensive. The company's Applied Science Group decided it could sell 200 machines "with the bulk of the machines to be used by scientists and engineers." IBM's Washington, D.C. office estimated that they could sell an additional 50 machines to government agencies.

In the end, over 1,800 of the 650s were made, making it by far the most successful computer system produced by that time. IBM was wrong about the number of 650s they could sell, and they were equally wrong about how customers would use the machine. While some customers did, in fact, use them for engineering and scientific work, other customers put the machines to work doing cost accounting, payrolls, inventory control, and even college admissions.

The world was becoming computerized, and IBM—right or wrong—was leading the way.

The Last of a Breed

The three computers shown here—the Remington UNIVAC-1 and the IBM models 701 and 650—were the first general-purpose computers. Despite their manufacturer's doubts, all three machines were very successful, and they helped to define the future shape of the computer industry. Ironically, while these machines broke much new ground—including the first use of magnetic tape, random-access memory (RAM), and alphanumeric input and output—these machines were the last of a breed. With the advent of the transistor, before long, these vacuum-tube–based computers would be on their way to the computer graveyard.

Smithsonian Institution
negative # 71-2641

The Remington UNIVAC-1 (1951) The UNIVAC-1 was built by ENIAC developers Presper Eckert and John Mauchly—the first product of their newly formed Eckert-Mauchly Computer Corporation. Before the UNIVAC was completed, their company was bought out by office equipment giant Remington-Rand. Remington initially intended to build only six UNIVACs, but more than forty were eventually sold.

The first UNIVAC-1 went into service at the U.S. Census Bureau, where it replaced the bureau's IBM punched-card system. According to legend, this angered IBM President Thomas Watson so much that he decided IBM should enter the computer business. The sixth UNIVAC-1 was purchased by General Electric, making it the first computer owned by a nongovernment organization.

UNIVAC's main computer unit is at the rear. The units on the right are magnetic tape storage units; the UNIVAC uses magnetized metal tape instead of the now-common plastic tape. One tape drive is used for program storage, another for data input, and others for data output. The operator's console and printer are on the left.

| 1947 | 1948 | 1949 | 1950 | **1951** |

Courtesy of IBM

The IBM Model 701 (1952) The IBM 701 was the first computer designed specifically for business use. The machine was manufactured in small modules that could be connected at the customer's site. Previous computers like the UNIVAC were assembled on-site in the customer's computer room; once installed, they were difficult to move.

The 701 contained a number of innovations, including 1,024 bits of random-access memory, a tape drive that used magnetized plastic tape, and a punched-card reader that allowed IBM customers to transfer their existing punched card data onto the computer.

Courtesy of IBM

The IBM 650 (1953) Introduced only two years after the 701, the 650 was a smaller, lower-cost machine, designed to appeal to customers who couldn't afford a 701. Although pessimistic IBM planners projected that the machine would only sell between 50 and 250 units, IBM eventually made nearly 2,000 of the 650s. One IBM executive nicknamed the 650 "IBM's Model T," because it was the first mass-produced computer.

Like the 701, the 650 could read from and write to both magnetic tape and punched cards. This flexibility appealed to IBM customers, who used the 650 for everything from engineering analysis to payroll processing. The 650 also set new standards for reliability, often continuously running for weeks at a time without incident.

| 1952 | 1953 | 1954 | 1955 | 1956 |

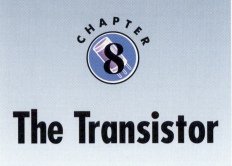

The Transistor

N 1964, MY father gave me a transistor radio for my birthday. I still remember that radio—it was a Monarch, made in Japan. It was built in a brown bakelite case about 4 inches square with a brass-colored speaker grill, and it had 18 transistors. On a good night, I could listen to Bruce "Cousin Brucie" Morrow's famous rock-and-roll show on WABC in New York City, 1,400 miles from my home in Miami. Every time I opened the radio to replace the 9-volt battery, I marveled that a handful of tiny metal cans (the transistors) could pick up signals from so far away.

Now, 30 years later, I'm typing this chapter on my trusty 80486-based laptop computer. The CPU chip alone has over 4 million transistors, but you'd need a microscope to see them—if they weren't buried inside a chunk of plastic. Once considered to be fragile, high-tech devices, transistors have become the basic building block of all modern electronic devices.

Virtually every electronic device constructed since the mid-1950s has used transistors instead of vacuum tubes—for several very good reasons. You can think of vacuum tubes and transistors as electronic booster pumps. If you put a weak electronic signal into one side of the pump, you get a much stronger signal out the other side. But as we saw earlier, vacuum tubes require a heater element (the filament) to get the electrons flowing. In many cases, the filament uses more power than the rest of the tube. For example, ENIAC used 18,000 tubes and consumed 100,000 watts of power. Of those 100,000 watts, more than 40,000 went to tube filaments, where the power was converted to heat. That heat had to be removed from ENIAC's room, leading to further power consumption.

Transistors are superior to vacuum tubes in many other ways. They are smaller—some are microscopic. Tubes, in contrast, are relatively large and are housed in a fragile glass envelope. Tubes don't stand up well to vibration—a sudden jolt will break either the glass or the near-molten glowing metal filament inside. Transistors are extremely rugged, and are virtually impervious to mechanical shock.

If you've ever owned a tube radio or television, you know that tubes require a warm-up period of between 30 seconds and a few minutes. This is because the *cathode*—the electron-emitting element inside the tube—must reach a certain temperature before it begins to produce a steady stream of electrons. Transistors need no warm-up period, so transistorized equipment "warms up" immediately.

Transistors operate at lower voltages than do tubes, making them more efficient for most uses. The portable radio I had before my Monarch transistor radio was an RCA tube portable. It used six batteries: Four 1.5-volt D batteries powered the tube filaments, and two 45-volt A batteries provided the 90 volts required by the tubes. The D batteries lasted about an hour, and the expensive A batteries about three hours, depending how loud I played the radio. The Monarch used one 9-volt square battery (called a "transistor battery" when it was first introduced), and that battery powered the radio for days on end.

Because transistors operate at lower voltages, the other components that make up an electronic circuit can be smaller, too. The result is that transistorized equipment is substantially smaller and lighter than a tube-based counterpart. Finally, transistors switch on and off faster than tubes, an important consideration if you're building a computer.

None of these advantages were lost on the computer engineers of the 1950s. When reliable transistors became available in the early 1950s, those engineers immediately scrapped their existing designs and started from scratch, using transistors in place of tubes. The next generation of computers would be far faster, cheaper, and more reliable than the previous generation.

The Transistor Age

The transistor may be the most significant single invention of the modern era. It was invented in 1946 by three scientists at AT&T's Bell Labs. As one of the terms of AT&T's antitrust exemption, the company had to license its patents to any company that wanted them. Even though the license was free to U.S.-based companies, there were very few takers at the beginning. One of the first overseas licensees was a tiny Japanese company called Tokyo Telecommunications Laboratory. The company was so small that it had trouble raising the $25,000 license fee—but it eventually came up with the money. You know that company today by its new name, chosen in 1956: Sony.

The First Transistor Although it looks like a prop from the Flintstones movie, this chunk of germanium crystal changed the world. It was invented in 1946 by John Bardeen, William Shockley, and Walter Brittain, research scientists at AT&T's Bell Laboratories. This prototype transistor was much larger than necessary; the large size made it easier to work with.

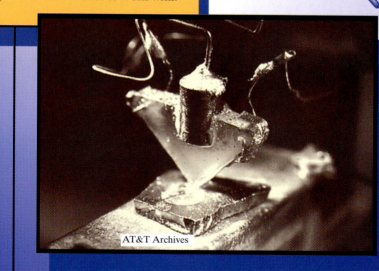

AT&T Archives

1945   **1946**   1947   1948   1949

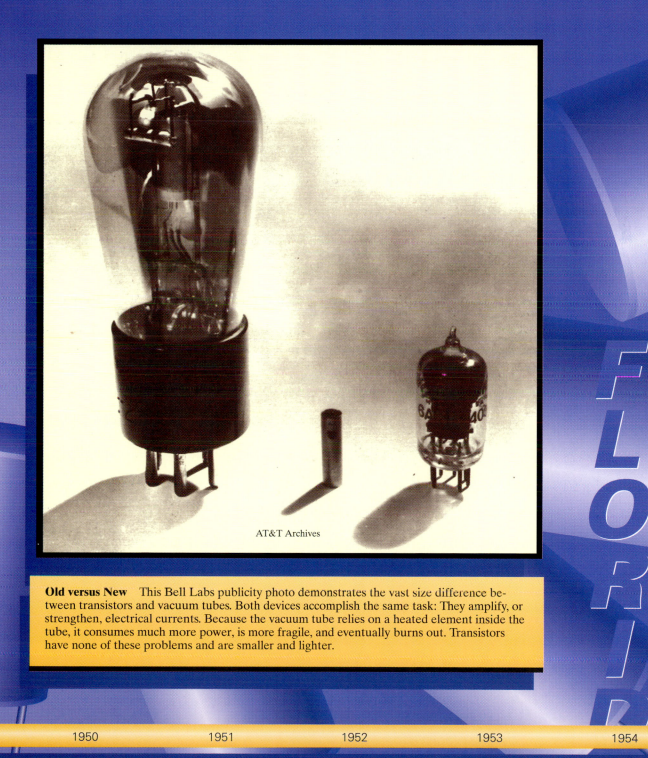

AT&T Archives

Old versus New   This Bell Labs publicity photo demonstrates the vast size difference between transistors and vacuum tubes. Both devices accomplish the same task: They amplify, or strengthen, electrical currents. Because the vacuum tube relies on a heated element inside the tube, it consumes much more power, is more fragile, and eventually burns out. Transistors have none of these problems and are smaller and lighter.

IBM Moves Ahead

THE TINY TRANSISTOR had a major impact on the fledgling computer industry. The transistor promised to solve many of the reliability and heat dissipation problems of the earlier generation of vacuum-tube computers. Further, transistor-based computers could be smaller and less expensive than their predecessors.

IBM and Sperry-Rand, the two market leaders, both began work on solid-state (all-transistor) computers in the mid-fifties. In 1959, IBM delivered four model 7090s to the United States Air Force for use in the Defense Early Warning (DEW) system. These computers were the first solid-state systems delivered to customers. A major attraction of the 7090 system was that it could use software developed for the older 709 and 704 systems, thus allowing customers to move up to the 7090 but still keep their existing software.

IBM's biggest competitor, Sperry-Rand (formerly Remington-Rand) also began work on a series of solid-state computers in the late fifties. Plagued by mismanagement and infighting, Sperry did not deliver their first machine until 1962. The UNIVAC III, when delivered, was entirely incompatible with earlier UNIVAC machines. UNIVAC customers had to rewrite all their software if they wanted to move up to the newest UNIVAC machine. Although it was 60 times faster than the UNIVAC I, the UNIVAC III was not a commercial success. The UNIVAC III was delivered a year late and by that time, IBM had moved far ahead of Sperry.

The success of the 7090 series and the smaller 1401 series solidified IBM's lead in the marketplace. The commercial success of these machines also produced a tremendous amount of cash for IBM, allowing the company to invest vast amounts of that cash in basic research and development. Although IBM was already far ahead of its competitors, its research and development machine kept running at full speed.

In 1964, after five years of development, IBM delivered a breakthrough product in the System/360, one of the most significant computers ever developed. IBM made a "bet the company" move in developing the System/360—the basic research and development costs ran well over a billion dollars. The System/360 development project was, up to that time, the largest privately financed research project ever done.

The System/360 wasn't a single system but a line of five computers designed to replace 15 existing IBM models. All System/360 machines were compatible with one another, and customers could move up from a smaller 360 to a larger machine as their needs dictated.

The System/360 project involved much more than just a new computer. Existing tape drives, card readers, memory devices, and printers weren't fast enough to keep up with the 360, so IBM redesigned those components as well. The System/360 line represented several technological breakthroughs in processing speed, memory technology, printing, and programming flexibility.

The System/360 was an immediate success, eventually earning many billions of dollars for IBM. Six months after its announcement in April of 1964, IBM had booked orders for System/360s that totalled more than three times IBM's entire annual income. The System/360 also had a chilling effect on competition in the computer industry; many smaller rival firms—notably General Electric and RCA—took one look at the technology in the 360 and decided to get out of the computer industry, further widening IBM's lead.

IBM's System/360

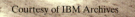
Courtesy of IBM Archives

The System/360 family of computers, introduced in 1964, was one of IBM's most profitable products. The 360 replaced 15 earlier computer models, none of which were compatible with one another. In their place, IBM introduced five different models of the 360, all of which were completely compatible with one another. IBM also developed software to allow programs written for earlier IBM machines to operate on the 360. This picture shows a typical System/360 installation with the processing unit, tape drives, and operator's console.

1960   1962   **1964**

JAN   FEB   MAR   APR   MAY   JUN

Fast computers need fast printers. In order to sell the System/360 into the growing business market, IBM needed a printer that could generate the mountains of utility bills, payroll checks, invoices, and financial statements required by their customers. The 1403 printer, introduced at the same time as the System/360, fulfilled that need. The 1403 used a revolving metal chain; each letter, number, and punctuation mark was represented by a link in the chain. The chain revolved continuously at a very high speed. To print a letter, the printer pushed out a metal rod at the desired print location just as the proper link passed by. These printers were dreadfully noisy but very effective: They could print 1,100 lines of text per minute. Many 1403s served into the 1980s, when laser printer technology finally made them obsolete.

The System/360 Model 1403 Chain Printer

Courtesy of IBM Archives

1966   1968   1970

JUL   AUG   SEP   OCT   NOV   DEC

Digital Equipment Corporation and the Minicomputer

BY 1968, IBM'S REVENUES approached $7 billion. The market for computing hardware, once thought to be limited to a select few government and educational markets, proved to be larger than anyone's wildest dreams.

IBM's strategy was to sell what the IBM sales staff called "Big Iron." Though the System/360 came in five sizes, even the smallest 360 was more computing iron than many companies could afford. IBM's competitors in the mainframe computer business—often called the "Seven Dwarves"—were outgunned by IBM at almost every turn.

In 1957 Digital Equipment Corporation was founded by Ken Olsen and Harlan Anderson, both former MIT computer engineers. Digital's initial product line was specialized digital logic circuits for the science and computer industries. Ironically, many of Digital's early products were used by other computer makers to design and test their own computers.

In 1960, Digital announced a small, high-speed computer called the PDP-1. Unlike its competitors, Digital offered very little support and software for the PDP-1. The machine was marketed to companies and universities who were sufficiently computer-literate to develop their own software. The PDP-1 was priced between $125,000 and $250,000, depending on options. This was an unbelievable price at a time when competitive systems began at $1 million.

Digital's machines and software were designed to require as little attention and maintenance as possible. While even the smallest System/360 needed a staff of attendants and operators, Digital's little PDP-1 could sit in a corner of the computer room, running 24 hours a day for weeks at a time.

The PDP-1 was an immediate success, and Digital continually expanded and improved its computer line. By the late 1960s, Digital's PDP-8 and PDP-10 computers competed head-to-head with virtually every IBM offering. Because they were less expensive to purchase and operate than IBM's offerings, many Digital machines found their way into university and high school computer laboratories. This trend had a very positive effect on Digital's image in the industry, since it created legions of programmers and computer scientists who cut their computing teeth on Digital machines.

By 1970, Digital's revenues were $142 million; by 1980 the company's revenues topped $2 billion, putting it in the coveted second-place seat behind IBM. Those Boston venture capitalists made out okay, too: They sold their Digital stock in 1968 and 1972 for over $400 million!

The First Small Computers

The Digital PDP-8 Computer

For thousands of baby-boomer computer users, the venerable PDP-8 was the first computer they ever used. First introduced in 1966, PDP-8s were installed by the thousands in small businesses, universities, high schools, newspapers, and book publishers. Digital also sold a large number of PDP-8s to Original Equipment Manufacturers (OEMs), who added their own customized software to create turn-key packages for their customers. By 1975, Digital had sold 40,000 PDP-8 systems. If a customer outgrew the PDP-8, it was a fairly simple matter to upgrade to Digital's large PDP-10 or PDP-11 system. Most PDP-8 software could run unmodified on the larger machines, and this kept customers loyal to Digital.

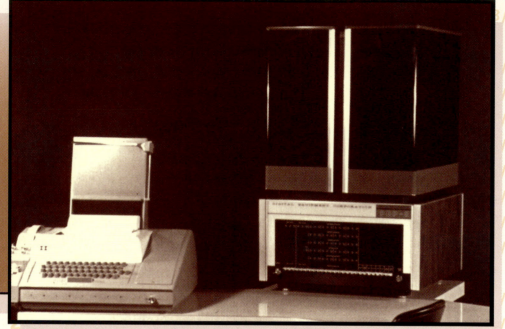

Courtesy of Digital EquipmentCorporation

The VT-52 Terminal (c. 1975)

All Digital Equipment systems supported the use of video display terminals, or VDTs. This model VT-52 was the first in a long line of inexpensive, high-quality, high-speed terminals from Digital. Unlike competitive systems, Digital made it easy to attach VDTs to their systems, and they developed sophisticated application software specifically for VDT applications. They also priced the VDT units at about half the cost of a comparable IBM unit. At the time, most competitive systems still used punched cards or magnetic tape as their only form of input and output. To give you an idea of the significance of the VDT, imagine trying to do word processing via punched cards!

Courtesy of DEC

1966   1967   1968   1969   1970

A Typical PDP-11 Installation
Digital's video terminals were relatively inexpensive, and many Digital customers took advantage by connecting as many users as possible to their Digital computers. The availability of video-based applications like word processing and spreadsheet programs brought millions of new users into the world of computing. With just a little training, people who knew nothing at all about computers could sit down at a terminal and do productive work.

Courtesy of DEC

As you can see, the computer market had turned into a race for second place.

Interestingly, most of the companies on this list are either gone or have merged.

Domestic Data Processing Revenues, 1963

Company	Revenue	Background
IBM	$1,244,161,000	IBM's gamble with the System/360 project paid off in a big way. As of the end of 1963, IBM's revenues from computer hardware topped $1 billion, nearly ten times that of Sperry, their nearest competitor.
Sperry-Rand	$145,480,000	Sperry-Rand bought RCA's floundering computer division in 1971, and merged with Burroughs to form Unisys in the late 1980s.
AT&T*	$97,000,000	AT&T acquired National Cash Register in 1992; the company now operates as the computer division of AT&T.
Control Data Corporation	$84,610,000	Control Data Corporation is still in business, but the company completely missed the boat when the world turned to small computers in the late 1980s.
Philco (division of Ford)	$73,900,000	Of all the companies on the list, only Philco is completely gone; the company was acquired by Ford Motor Company in 1961. Philco specialized in lightweight transistorized computer equipment for military and aerospace use. Philco doubtless owes its number 5 place on the list to the fact that its customers had very deep pockets.
Burroughs	$42,145,000	Burroughs formed Unisys in the late 1980s.
General Electric	$38,600,000	GE's computer division was bought by Honeywell in the late 1960s.
National Cash Register	$30,718,000	NCR was acquired by AT&T in 1992
Honeywell	$27,000,000	Honeywell bought most of GE's computer division in the late 1960s.

*AT&T was not considered one of the Seven Dwarves because it was actually bigger than IBM due to its income from telephone operations.

CHAPTER 11

Data Communications

F YOU'VE EVER used an automated teller machine (ATM), an online information service, or a credit card verification terminal, you can thank Emile Baudot. Monsieur Baudot was a nineteenth century French telegraph engineer who solved a very important problem of his day. The problem was how to send more than one telegraph conversation on a single telegraph line at one time. Applications of his ingenious solution are still with us today.

Telegraphs of Baudot's day used a system devised by American inventor Samuel F.B. Morse. The Morse system used human operators to send and receive telegraph messages using a series of dots and dashes. The transmitting operator would tap out the message in dots and dashes on a telegraph key, and the receiving operator would listen to and copy down the message at the receiving end. As mentioned, one major shortcoming of the Morse system was that it could only carry one message at a time.

In 1874, Baudot perfected a system called the multiplex telegraph, which allowed up to eight telegraph messages to share a single telegraph line. Baudot's machine contained a number of technological breakthroughs. It was the first electronic communication device to use a typewriter-style keyboard, a tradition that continues to this day. Because Baudot's machines were designed to communicate with one another—and not with a human operator—they did not use Morse code. Instead, Baudot devised a code that sent five pulses of equal length down the wire for each character transmitted. The machines themselves did the encoding and decoding, eliminating the need for operators to become proficient at Morse code.

Many of Baudot's ideas are essential to modern-day computing. Baudot invented the concept of *serial data*—sending information over a wire as a string of binary 1s and 0s—that is the fundamental element of most computer communications. The Baudot code was used well into the 1970s, most notably on the worldwide TELEX teletypewriter network and on the Associated Press (AP) and United Press International (UPI) newswires.

Early computer makers needed a way to get text data into and out of their computers, and the teletypewriter served that function well. The ENIAC, UNIVAC, and other early machines used mechanical teletypewriter machines as their keyboard and printer mechanisms.

As computer technology progressed, a new technique called *timesharing* made it possible to connect several teletypewriter terminals to one computer, thus spreading the computer's power among several users. The remote terminals were connected to the host computer via special leased telephone lines. These phone lines were different from ordinary phone lines in that they were designed to carry the on-and-off pulses of digital data, rather than the varying voltage of a voice telephone line. While leased lines work well for computer communications, they are expensive and inflexible.

In the early 1960s, engineers at AT&T's Bell Laboratories devised a way to convert a computer's digital data into a form that can be carried by ordinary voice-grade telephone lines. Their invention is the *modem* (MOdulator-DEModulator), and it revolutionized computer communications. A modem converts a computer's digital data into a series of varying tones. The tones can travel over a telephone circuit to another modem, where they are converted back into digital data. Using a modem, computer users can connect a terminal to virtually any telephone line.

The flexibility provided by the modem opened up a whole new world of computing—one that is still expanding today. Released from the constraints imposed by expensive leased lines, companies could place computer terminals any place they were needed. This allowed large national companies to connect all of their field offices.

The modem benefited small companies, too. Companies too small to buy their own computer could buy computer time from computer timesharing services. Timesharing services provided the terminals, modems, and host computer, allowing small companies to enter the computer age at minimal expense and with little or no long-term commitment.

Data Communications

The science of data communications predates the computer itself. Early digital communication techniques date back to the nineteenth century, when Frenchman Emile Baudot devised a way to send several simultaneous telegraph messages over a single telegraph line. Baudot's techniques have been improved and expanded, but the basic technology he created is still with us today.

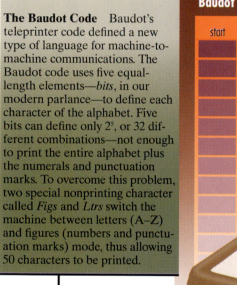

The Baudot Code Baudot's teleprinter code defined a new type of language for machine-to-machine communications. The Baudot code uses five equal-length elements—*bits*, in our modern parlance—to define each character of the alphabet. Five bits can define only 2^5, or 32 different combinations—not enough to print the entire alphabet plus the numerals and punctuation marks. To overcome this problem, two special nonprinting character called *Figs* and *Ltrs* switch the machine between letters (A–Z) and figures (numbers and punctuation marks) mode, thus allowing 50 characters to be printed.

Baudot Code (yellow denotes positive current)

start	1	2	3	4	5	stop	shift LETTERS	shift FIGURES
							A	-
							B	?
							C	:
							D	$
							E	3
							F	!
							G	&
							H	#
							I	8
							J	bell
							K	(
							L	)
								*

1870   **1874**   1890   1910   1930

How a Modem Works   A *modem* (short for MOdulator-DEModulator) bridges the digital world of the computer and the analog world of the telephone network. Because telephone lines are designed to carry the human voice, they cannot carry the rapid on-and-off pulses of digital data. A modem solves this problem by converting the computer's on-and-off pulses into a series of varying tones. Early modems could only transfer 300 bits (about 30 characters) per second, but modern-day modems can achieve speeds up to 28,800 bits (about 2,900 characters) per second.

A Timesharing Service
Timesharing services provide computer services to companies that don't have their own computer. A typical timesharing network may have hundreds or even thousands of terminals connected via modems. Users connect to the host computer with terminals attached to modems. Timesharing services were very popular in the 1960s and 1970s, since they allowed smaller companies to gain computer power without making a large investment in equipment and personnel.

1950   1970

TWO GUYS IN A GARAGE: THE FIRST COMPUTER STARTUP COMPANIES

CONTENTS

OVERVIEW

DIGITAL COMPUTERS CONSIST of electronic switches. The more powerful the computer, the more switches required. Until 1958, only two types of electronic switch were available: the vacuum tube and the transistor. While a transistor has many advantages over a tube, they share one major disadvantage. Tubes and transistors are discrete components; that is, each tube or transistor can only switch one circuit at a time. In a circuit with hundreds of electronic switches, there are literally thousands of wires—each one placed by hand—that connect the tubes or transistors. The complexity of the wiring increased the cost of early computers. And because there were so many wires in discrete component computers, the possibility for miswiring or failure was very high.

When transistors became available in the early 1950s, they reduced the size and power consumption of computers, but the wiring complexity remained. The introduction of printed circuit boards in the 1950s reduced the amount of wiring required, but each individual transistor still had to be physically connected to another.

In 1958, Robert Noyce and Jack Kilby—two inventors at two different companies—created a device we now know as the integrated circuit, or semiconductor chip. An integrated circuit is a single piece of material—usually silicon—that contains dozens, hundreds, or (in the case of modern microprocessors) millions of transistors.

Advances in integrated circuit technology eventually led to the creation of the microprocessor chip. Early microprocessors were misleadingly called "computers on a chip." This isn't exactly true, since microprocessors don't typically include memory, input and output circuits, and other peripheral circuits necessary for a complete working computer. Still, the microprocessor contained enough circuitry to build a relatively small computer for little cost.

The impact of the microprocessor is still being felt today. Creation of the early microprocessors led directly and immediately to the development of desktop computers. These computers weren't created by big companies like IBM and NCR, but by small entrepreneurial outfits with two or three employees. In fact, the big computer companies completely misjudged the power of the microprocessor—largely because they had a huge investment in their existing product lines.

The best known of these new, small companies was a tiny outfit called Apple Computer. The early history of Apple is a sort of high-tech David and Goliath story, and the two founders—Steve Jobs and Steve Wozniak—have become industry legends. Their success is so widely known that even today, small startup computer companies are often referred to as "two guys in a garage."

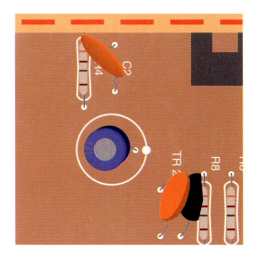

CHAPTER

The Integrated Circuit

AS WE'VE SEEN, today's computer technology couldn't exist without the transistor. The transistor greatly reduced the physical size and power requirements of computers while increasing their speed and reliability. But as computers became more complex and used more and more transistors, another obstacle appeared. Each element in a computer—each transistor, resistor, capacitor, and other electronic component—had to be connected to another element.

Each element in a circuit was connected by a piece of wire and each wire had to be cut, placed, and soldered by hand. In a solid-state computer with 100,000 transistors, there would be 300,000 connections (transistors have three connections).

A partial solution was devised by the National Bureau of Standards during World War II. NBS engineers—working on a proximity detonator for artillery shells—devised a new method of electronic assembly called the printed circuit. Instead of making each connection by an individual wire, the NBS engineers mounted each component on a thin piece of bakelite. Thin copper lines printed on the board connected the components. The copper lines were created by a lithographic process, allowing for fast and accurate reproduction of large numbers of identical circuit boards.

Printed circuits were cheaper and more reliable than hand wiring, and the printed circuit board quickly found its way into many commercial and consumer applications. By the early 1950s the printed circuit had largely replaced the old-fashioned hand-wiring method.

In 1958, two engineers at two competing companies took the printed circuit approach one radical step further. Instead of mounting individual transistors on a printed circuit board and connecting them, why not make one piece of silicon with many transistors already connected into a useful configuration? Robert Noyce at Fairchild and Jack Kilby at Texas Instruments both created integrated circuits, or simply *chips*, at about the same time. After a protracted patent battle, Kilby was issued a patent covering the basic integrated circuit, and Noyce was credited for inventing a method to interconnect the components on a chip.

Legal complications aside, the integrated circuit, or IC, again revolutionized the entire electronics industry. Virtually all modern electronics—from hearing aids to cellular telephones to computers—use IC technology.

Electronic Building Blocks

The development of new electronic devices like the transistor and the integrated circuit inspired new and innovative ways of building equipment. These pictures show the evolution of electronic construction since World War II.

The Printed Circuit Board The earliest electronic equipment—primarily radio equipment—was constructed by mounting components on a metal chassis and connecting the components with wire. Building things this way was time consuming and susceptible to human error.

  The first major advance in electronic construction was the printed circuit board, or PC board. First introduced during World War II, the PC board was originally used for military applications. In this method of construction, all the components are mounted on a thin bakelite or fiberglass board. Electronic conductors called *traces* connect the components. The traces are etched onto the board using a lithographic process, allowing the production of hundreds or thousands of identical boards. More complex circuit designs may have two sets of traces, one on each side of the board. PC boards are still very labor-intensive, since each component must be placed by hand.

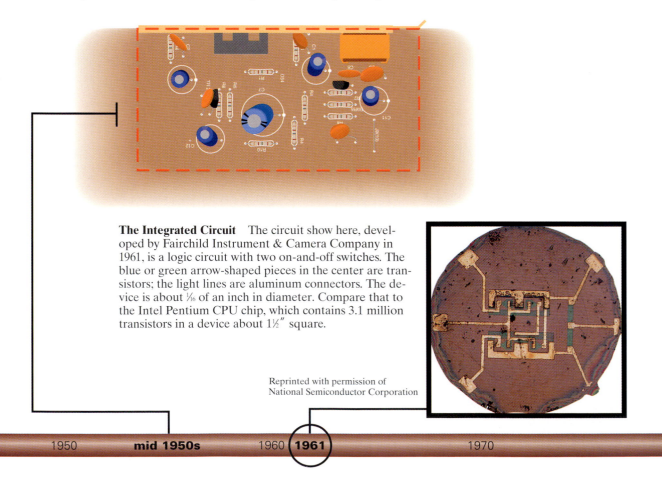

The Integrated Circuit The circuit show here, developed by Fairchild Instrument & Camera Company in 1961, is a logic circuit with two on-and-off switches. The blue or green arrow-shaped pieces in the center are transistors; the light lines are aluminum connectors. The device is about ¹⁄₁₆ of an inch in diameter. Compare that to the Intel Pentium CPU chip, which contains 3.1 million transistors in a device about 1½″ square.

Reprinted with permission of
National Semiconductor Corporation

1950   **mid 1950s**   1960 **1961**   1970

Integrated Circuits on a Printed Circuit Board Most modern electronic equipment is built using a combination of integrated circuit and printed circuit board techniques. Each chip has a number of pins protruding from the bottom of the chip. (The pins are the connections to the circuitry inside the chip.) The chips are mounted on the printed circuit board with their pins passing through holes drilled in the board. The pins are then soldered into place by a machine. Some printed circuit boards have traces on both sides, and others may have 5 or 6 layers of traces in a "sandwich."

Surface Mounting The latest electronic construction technique is called "surface mounting." Unlike conventional PC boards, surface mount boards have no drilled holes. The components are heat-welded or soldered into place directly on the traces on the board. This technique allows for the use of smaller components than those of conventional PC boards, and is exceptionally well-suited to automated assembly.

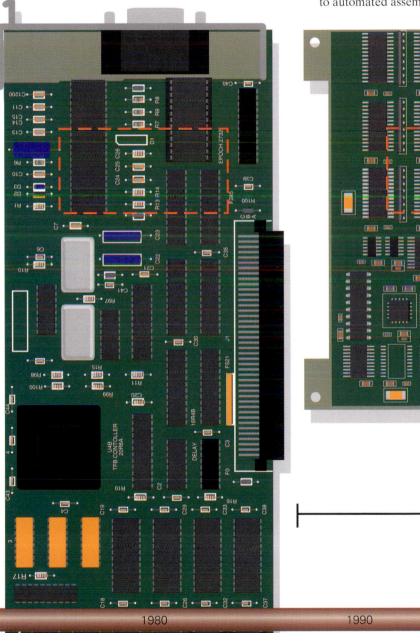

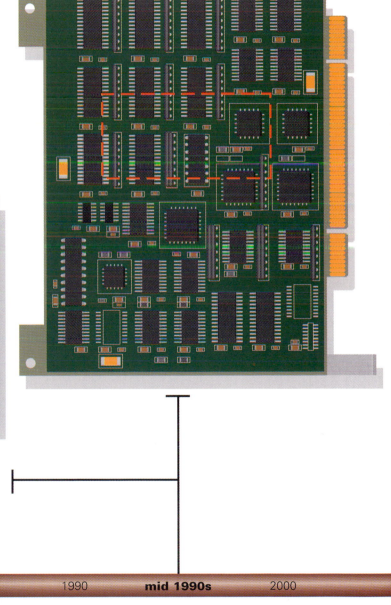

1980   1990   **mid 1990s**   2000

CHAPTER

13

Early Microprocessors

I N 1968, ROBERT NOYCE left Fairchild to start his own company. Noyce and fellow Fairchild engineers Andy Grove and Gordon Moore founded their company, Intel, to produce integrated circuits. A few months later, the fledgling company was approached by Busicom, a Japanese company that specialized in scientific calculators. Busicom's engineers had designed a new electronic calculator, but they needed Intel's chipmaking abilities to turn their plans into a finished product.

The original Busicom design called for a group of 12 integrated circuits on a printed circuit board. Intel engineer Ted Hoff had a better and more radical idea. Hoff proposed to build a single-chip computer that could be programmed to act as a calculator.

The result was the Intel 4004, the first microprocessor chip. The 4004 contained over 2,000 transistors on a 3 millimeter-by-4 millimeter silicon chip. The 4004 could perform 60,000 operations per second—as much computing power as the ENIAC. Busicom's engineers were thrilled with the 4004, and the company eventually sold over 100,000 4004-based desktop calculators.

Intel, sensing a wider market for the 4004, negotiated with Busicom to buy the rights to the 4004, and the Japanese company finally accepted a one-time payment of $60,000 in exchange for exclusive rights to the 4004 design. Intel made the chip available to the public in 1971. The $200 chip was quickly and widely adopted into thousands of applications.

The 4004 was a 4-bit computer, meaning that it could process 4 bits of information at a time. By contrast, today's high-powered PCs use 32- and 64-bit microprocessors. Intel realized that a market existed for a more powerful microprocessor, and the company introduced the 8-bit 8008 processor in 1972. The 8008 was essentially an 8-bit version of the 4004, and its instruction set (the internal language used by the microprocessor) was, like that of the 4004, oriented toward mathematical functions.

In 1974, Intel announced the creation of the 8080 microprocessor. The 8080 was also an 8-bit chip, but it had a much larger instruction set than its predecessor did. While the 8008 required 20 additional chips to produce a working computer, the 8080 design needed only 6 chips. More importantly, the 4004 could only operate with 4 kilobytes of memory; the 8080 could handle 64 kilobytes. The original 8080 performed 1 million instructions per second and cost $360. As we'll see in the next chapter, the 8080, along with competitive chips from Mostek and Motorola, formed the foundation of the personal computer industry.

The Intel 4004 and the Pioneer 10 Spacecraft

The microprocessor, or "computer on a chip," went virtually unnoticed by the mainstream computer industry when it was first announced in 1971. Ten years later, the tiny microprocessor chip had rearranged an entire industry. The microprocessor combines all the essential elements of a computer—a processor, memory, and input/output circuits—on one small piece of silicon.

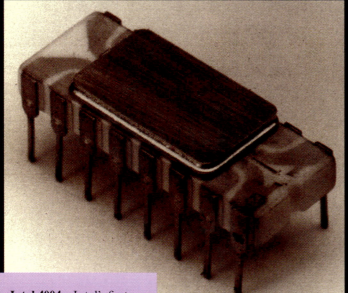

A Modern Microprocessor
In 1973, Intel chairman Gordon Moore predicted that the number of transistors on a microprocessor would double every 18 months. Moore's prediction became known in the industry as "Moore's Law," and it has held true for over 20 years. The Intel Pentium, introduced in 1993, illustrates just how far microprocessor technology has advanced in the past 20 years. The Pentium contains 3.1 million transistors, and can perform 90 million operations per second, or about 1,500 times the speed of the 4004.

The Intel 4004 Intel's first microprocessor was the Intel 4004, a 4-bit computer on a chip. It could process 4 bits of information at a time. By contrast, today's high-powered PCs use 32- and 64-bit microprocessors. The 4004 performed 60,000 instructions per second; today's fastest PCs can perform 100 million operations per second!

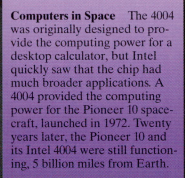

Computers in Space The 4004 was originally designed to provide the computing power for a desktop calculator, but Intel quickly saw that the chip had much broader applications. A 4004 provided the computing power for the Pioneer 10 spacecraft, launched in 1972. Twenty years later, the Pioneer 10 and its Intel 4004 were still functioning, 5 billion miles from Earth.

C H A P T E R

14

Early Personal Computers

THE PERSONAL COMPUTER age officially began in January of 1974. That month, *Popular Electronics* magazine featured the MITS Altair computer on the cover. MITS founder Ed Roberts decided to market a computer kit based on the Intel 8080. Offering the computer in a kit allowed MITS to enter the computer business with only minimal manufacturing facilities, and helped to keep the costs of the computer down—to $397. It also meant potential customers had to solder hundreds of chips and other components into place.

Through a stroke of good luck, Roberts was contacted by Les Solomon, the technical editor of *Popular Electronics*. Solomon was looking for a computer-related story for the January issue of the magazine, and he decided to put the Altair on the cover.

Within a few weeks, MITS had booked orders for over 4,000 Altair kits. MITS wasn't prepared for this onslaught of orders, and customers who had been promised delivery in two months found themselves waiting six months or more. One such customer was Bill Millard, president of IMS Associates, a small consulting company.

Millard had a contract to build a computer networking system for automobile dealerships, and he was way behind schedule. He needed several Altair computers right away. Frustrated by the long delivery time for the Altair, Millard decided to build his own computer—the IMSAI 8080. As long as he was building them, Millard figured that he might as well offer his machine for sale to the public, too. Millard took out a small ad in *Popular Electronics*, and before long the orders began to pour in, just like they had at MITS.

The IMSAI and Altair machines were, as you might expect, very similar. Both used an Intel 8080, and both machines had a front panel covered with lights and switches. They were also alike in what they didn't have: Neither machine had a keyboard, video display, disk drive, or tape storage unit.

Despite their shortcomings, the Altair and IMSAI caused a major stir in the computer industry. With a little work and patience, a buyer could have a functioning computer system for under $500. At the time, "real" small computers like the Digital Equipment Corporation PDP-11 cost at least $10,000, so buyers were more than willing to overlook the shortcomings of the new 8080-based computers.

Altair: A Dream System circa 1977

The MITS Altair was produced by a small firm in Albuquerque, New Mexico. MITS had been a pioneer of the electronic calculator business, but had been badly battered when giants like Texas Instruments and Hewlett-Packard entered the calculator business. First offered for sale in 1975, the Altair 8800 was the first computer specifically designed for the hobbyist market. The Altair used an Intel 8080 microprocessor chip, which was capable of controlling up to 64 kilobytes of memory. This was only a theoretical number, since memory was very expensive, and many hobbyists made do with the 256 bytes of memory supplied as standard equipment.

The original Altair had no keyboard, no video display, and no storage device. Users would enter their programs (in 8080 assembly language) one instruction at a time, using the switches on the front panel. Once the program was loaded, red lights on the front panel indicated the results of the program.

The system shown here is a later model Altair 8800b, introduced in 1977. The 8800b had a serial interface, which allowed the connection of a video display terminal and printer.

The Teletype Corporation model ASR-33 (circa 1960) was a combination keyboard, printer, and paper tape machine. It was originally designed for use as a news wire service printer, telex terminal, and private leased-line communications terminal. Many thousands of ASR-33s were built, and old, worn-out ASR-33s often found a second life as a terminal on an Altair.

The keyboard and printer could be used for input and output, saving the user from the tedium of using the Altair's front panel. As a bonus, programs could be stored and reloaded using the ASR-33's paper tape punch and reader. These machines were slow (10 characters per second) and noisy (you've heard them on countless radio and TV news broadcasts), and they always smelled of machine oil, but they were also as sturdy as a rock.

A used ASR-33 in good condition could cost as much as $700. Buyers with deep pockets could buy a brand-new ASR-33 direct from Teletype Corporation for $1,100—about twice the price of the Altair computer itself.

For our 1977 dream machine, we've chosen the Lear-Siegler ADM-3A video display terminal. The ADM-3A could display 24 lines of 80 characters each, a standard that is still with us today. The terminal's main circuit board filled the bottom of the ADM-3A's large cabinet.

The ADM-3A was originally offered fully assembled, but repeated requests from computer hobbyists led the company to offer a kit version. Like the Teletype, the terminal often cost more than the computer itself. In 1977, an ADM-3A kit was $995; the fully assembled version cost $1,195.

1975   1976   **1977**   1978   1979

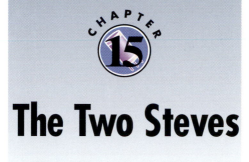

The Two Steves

LIKE MANY SAN FRANCISCO Bay area computer enthusiasts, Steve Jobs and Steve Wozniak first met at an early meeting of the Homebrew Computer Club. Wozniak, or "Woz," was an engineer at Hewlett-Packard. Jobs worked part-time at Atari, the computer games company.

Although the two had many differences, they shared an intense interest in small computers. Woz, the engineer, was extremely interested in computer hardware. Jobs was trying to find a way to turn his passion for computers into a profit.

Woz had designed a single-board computer around the Motorola 6800 microprocessor. While the 6800 was fairly powerful, it was also fairly expensive at $175. In 1976, a small company called MOS Technology announced a pin-for-pin replacement for the 6800 called the 6502. Although it performed many of the same functions as the 6800, it cost only $25.

Woz purchased a 6502 chip and immediately began work on a programming language— BASIC—for the new chip. Once the programming was complete, Woz redesigned his original 6800-based computer to accommodate the new 6502 chip. He and Jobs named the machine the Apple computer. Working from Jobs's garage, Woz designed circuitry to connect a video monitor and keyboard to the computer. Jobs and Wozniak took the prototype computer—packaged in an aluminum briefcase—to several manufacturers, hoping that one of them might be interested enough to license their design. Two engineers at IMSAI were very interested, but IMSAI was in complete disarray at the time, and the engineers wisely suggested that Jobs and Wozniak might be better off on their own.

By the end of 1976, Wozniak had designed and built a much-improved computer, the Apple II. The Apple II was a single-board computer like the Apple I, but the Apple II went several steps farther. The Apple II had the BASIC programming language built in, and it also had the ability to display text and graphics in color.

The two Steves once again set out to find a way to bring their product to the market. Nolan Bushnell, Jobs's boss at Atari, referred the two Steves to Don Valentine, a local venture capitalist. Valentine thought the venture was too risky, and put the two in touch with Mike Markulla, a retired (at age 32!) Intel executive. Markulla visited Jobs's garage and was very impressed with what he saw.

Within a few months of their meeting, Jobs, Wozniak, and Markulla formalized their arrangement. They formed a company, Apple Computer, with each of the three owning one-third of the stock. Markulla put up $91,000 for operating capital, and the company was on its way.

The Apple II remained in production for over 15 years, a remarkable lifespan for any product. Ironically, the longevity of the Apple II eventually led to a split between the two Steves. Wozniak designed a third version of the Apple called the Apple III, but the machine was too expensive and never caught on with buyers. Wozniak left Apple to enjoy his new-found fortune. Jobs championed a completely new line of computers, eventually heading up the team that designed the Macintosh computer (covered in Chapter 18).

The Apple I and II

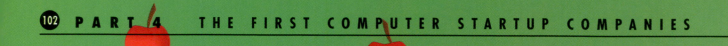

APPLE COMP...
CONFIDENTIAL

The Apple I   The Apple I used a Mostek 6502 microprocessor and had 4 kilobytes of memory. Because floppy disks weren't readily available, the Apple I used an ordinary cassette tape recorder for program and data storage. The machine didn't have a case or power supply—buyers were expected to provide their own.

After completing the prototype, Woz gave away detailed plans for building the machine, which a few intrepid hobbyists followed. The machine in this picture—hand-assembled by Wozniak—is now on display at the Smithsonian.

All photos courtesy of Apple Computer, Inc.

1976

The Two Steves   This photograph, taken around 1976, shows the two Steves (Jobs on the right, Wozniak on the left) with the Apple I prototype. Differences with each other and with Apple chairman John Sculley eventually led both Steves away from Apple.

The Apple IIe   The Apple IIe was Apple's workhorse computer for many years. The machine used the same Mostek 6502 microprocessor as the earlier Apple I, and could hold up to 64 kilobytes of memory. The Apple II had a built-in keyboard and power supply, and seven expansion slots. Third-party manufacturers made a wide array of plug-in cards for the Apple II, allowing the machine to be used for everything from game playing to scientific data acquisition.

The Apple II was very popular with buyers, since even a nontechnical user could unpack, set up, and operate the machine within a few minutes. Millions of Apple IIs were built, and many of them are still in use today.

THE PC GROWS UP

CONTENTS

BY 1981, THE microcomputer industry had grown to nearly a billion dollar business. Hundreds of companies had joined the fray, ranging from small startups trying to re-create the magic of Jobs's garage to huge international companies like Texas Instruments and Xerox.

From a buyer's point of view, the industry was a mess. Dozens of vendors offered hundreds of models of computers. Prices ranged from a few hundred dollars for Commodore's entry-level PET computer to tens of thousands for Cromemco's System III small business computer.

Choosing and using a computer required a major investment of time and money, since it was virtually impossible to use a microcomputer system without learning the inner workings of the machine first. Even if you did manage to get your system installed and working, the hardware and software were frequently unreliable.

The software industry wasn't in much better shape. The vast majority of computers sold between 1975 and 1980 (with the notable exception of the Apple II) used Digital Research's CP/M operating system. CP/M promised a degree of compatibility between systems, but each manufacturer used a different and incompatible type of floppy disk. As a result, a program or data file created on a Brand X computer wouldn't work on a Brand Y machine.

Seeing a major opportunity in the making, IBM commissioned a top-secret development team—led by IBM veterans Bill Lowe and Don Estridge—to develop a professional, reliable personal computer. Project Acorn, as the team was known, operated from an obscure IBM facility in Boca Raton, Florida. Lowe and Estridge were given 13 months to deliver a next-generation personal computer. To keep the IBM bureaucracy out of the way, they reported directly to IBM president John Opel—an unprecedented breach of IBM's rigid corporate structure.

The Project Acorn team delivered as promised, and IBM entered the small computer business in August of 1981. Competitors were stunned—not by the technology in the IBM machine, but by the attention to detail that pervaded every aspect of IBM's offering. In 13 months, IBM had created not just a new computer, but an entire system that included monitors, printers, expansion cards, and a full range of software. The IBM machines carried an air of professionalism unknown in the industry.

In another un-IBM-like move, the company decided to make the IBM PC an "open" machine. IBM had previously kept technical details to themselves, making it difficult for other companies to design accessory products for IBM machines. Emulating the open architecture of Apple's machines, IBM published detailed technical specifications for the PC, making it easy for third-party hardware and software developers to design add-on products for the IBM PC. Within months, a thriving industry developed around the IBM PC, with dozens of companies providing accessory products.

The IBM Personal Computer

ON AUGUST 12, 1981, the personal computer industry—not yet a decade old—changed forever. On that day, mainframe computer giant IBM announced their own personal computer. The announcement had been rumored for months. Many in the industry thought that IBM—known for its high-quality systems, legendary customer support, and in-your-face business tactics—couldn't possibly create a personal computer. IBM, they said, was too large, too bureaucratic, and too slow to deal with the fast-changing world of personal computers. Others saw the move as inevitable. Apple Computer—at the time the largest maker of small computers—placed a full-page ad in dozens of newspapers nationwide, welcoming IBM to the business. IBM's arrival, Apple maintained, underscored the fact that personal computers were important and not just a passing fad.

In typical IBM fashion, the company wrote their own rulebook for entry into the PC marketplace. Their machines would not be sold through IBM's traditional network of blue-suited salespeople, but would instead be sold at the retail level by a select group of dealers. Specifically, IBM systems would be available from only two sources: ComputerLand, with its nationwide network of stores, and Sears Business Systems Centers.

While IBM was writing new rules, they were also breaking a few of their own. No other IBM product had ever been built using outside contractors. IBM's design team, given only a little more than a year to produce the machine, had been given permission to go outside the company for whatever parts they needed. As a result, the IBM Personal Computer was built with parts made almost entirely outside IBM. Even the operating system software—a crucial component of any new computer system—had been farmed out.

The original IBM Personal Computer was, in many ways, a technologically unremarkable machine. The computer used Intel's 8088 microprocessor, a 16-bit descendant of the 8080. The choice of microprocessors seemed strange, since the 8088 was essentially a cheaper version of Intel's 8086 processor. The 8086 and 8088 were very similar and ran the same software, but the 8088 was slower. Neither the 8086 or 8088 could run 8080 software, so the growing library of existing 8080 programs would have to be rewritten to run on the IBM machine.

The IBM PC, as it almost immediately became called, came with 16 kilobytes of memory. Options were available to expand the memory up to 256 kilobytes. The machine could hold two floppy-disk drives, each holding 160 kilobytes of data. Two video displays were available, one monochrome and one color.

The PC was priced at $2,495 for the basic model with 16 kilobytes of memory and one floppy-disk drive, similar in cost to an Apple II. Filling out the memory to the full 256 kilobytes added another $1,000, and a color monitor added $750.

Two operating systems were available for the new machine. One was CP/M-86, an 8086 version of the popular CP/M operating system. The other was IBM PC-DOS, a new CP/M-like operating system from Microsoft. This intrigued many people, since Microsoft had previously produced programming languages and application programs, not operating systems. Although IBM executives expressed no preference for one operating system over the other, the price list said it all: PC-DOS was $40, CP/M-86 was $180.

IBM had done their homework, and they knew that a new personal computer, even one bearing the IBM nameplate, could not succeed without a wide library of software. Months before the announcement, IBM, under a thick veil of secrecy, had given prototype IBM Personal Computers to key software companies. As a result, IBM was able to announce a large variety of application programs for the PC from day one, including the leading word processor, spreadsheet, and database manager programs.

IBM had set an ambitious goal for the PC: From the day of the announcement through the last day of 1981, they proposed to sell 100,000 machines. Production snafus—many caused by lack of coordination among the dozens of suppliers involved—held the actual number to 65,000 units for the first year.

The IBM PC: A Dream System, circa 1982

First released in 1981, the IBM PC used an Intel 8088 processor. The PC could hold up to 256 kilobytes of memory, four times the capacity of the Apple II. The original PC came with one or two floppy drives, but an expanded model—the IBM Personal Computer/XT—was introduced a few months later, offering an improved keyboard and optional hard disk. IBM offered the PC with two different display options. The machine shown here is connected to an IBM color monitor, but most early PCs were equipped with the less expensive (and sharper) monochrome display. An extensive advertising campaign made sure that everyone in America knew about IBM's small computers. Many of the early IBM PC buyers were people who had never even considered owning a computer before.

1982

The Software Explosion

TODAY'S COMPUTER USERS often take software for granted. Most PCs now come with an assortment of pre-installed software. For many users, that software is all they need, but if your needs go beyond the basics, you can choose from tens of thousands of software titles from hundreds of software companies.

It wasn't always so. The original MITS Altair had a bank of switches and lights on the front panel. To program the computer, users entered programs as binary data—one step at a time—using the switches. Once the program was entered, a series of red lights—also in binary—indicated the results of the program. The entire process was very slow and tedious, and one wrong switch setting would cause the computer to crash, requiring the user to start all over again.

MITS founder Ed Roberts realized that he needed a programming language to make the Altair easier to use. At the time, a relatively new language called *BASIC* was becoming very popular. BASIC (for Beginner's All-purpose Symbolic Instruction Code) had been designed at Dartmouth College in 1967 as a simple way to teach programming. BASIC had become very popular with college students, since it allowed them to create relatively complex programs with a minimal amount of computer knowledge.

Two students at Harvard University—Bill Gates and Paul Allen—decided to write a version of BASIC that would run on the Altair. The only problem was that they didn't *have* an Altair, since the only functioning Altair was the prototype at MITS headquarters.

Undaunted by this small detail, Gates and Allen set out to write their BASIC program. They began by writing an 8080 simulator program to run on Harvard's PDP-10 minicomputer. The simulator program mimicked the operation of the 8080, essentially making a $250,000 Digital Equipment Corporation minicomputer operate like a $397 Altair.

In 1974, after working day and night for eight weeks, they completed what would come to be known as Microsoft BASIC. Allen took the program to MITS headquarters in Albuquerque to test it on the "real" Altair. The program worked flawlessly the first time. MITS licensed BASIC from Gates and Allen, and for a time the two moved to Albuquerque and worked as contract programmers for MITS.

Microsoft BASIC soon became the de facto standard programming language for small computers. Ironically, Gates and Allen didn't initially make much money from BASIC. Software was so scarce in those early days that computer users shared whatever software they had, paying little or no attention to legal details like copyrights. At one point, Gates considered selling the rights to BASIC to MITS for less than $10,000.

With the availability of Microsoft BASIC, small computer owners found a tool to create useful software for their computers. A few entrepreneurs began to write application programs in BASIC for sale to other computer owners. Before long, a small industry of software developers emerged, providing everything from accounting software to statistical analysis programs in BASIC.

The popularity of its version of BASIC led Microsoft to develop compilers for other computer languages, including FORTRAN, COBOL, and Pascal. (A compiler is a program that translates a programming language into a machine-usable code.) In 1980, IBM chose Microsoft as the primary language provider for the then-unannounced Project Acorn. Gates convinced IBM to let Microsoft provide the operating system for the PC, and IBM agreed. Gates had offered a piece of software he hadn't written yet, but Microsoft bought a program called QDOS (for Quick & Dirty DOS) from a small company in Seattle. Microsoft's programmers modified QDOS to run on the IBM hardware, and Microsoft's operating systems empire was born.

Today, Microsoft owns the lion's share of the operating systems market. Former competitor Digital Research is long gone, and former ally IBM is now a competitor.

The Software Explosion

The history of the computer software industry is dominated by one company: Microsoft. Virtually all of Microsoft's early competitors—notably Digital Research, inventors of the CP/M operating system—have disappeared. Today, Microsoft is the largest software company in the world, and founders Bill Gates and Paul Allen are billionaires.

Microsoft BASIC

Gates and Allen complete Microsoft BASIC for the Altair. Although several other companies had promised to deliver a working BASIC program to MITS, Gates and Allen complete the task first by working day and night for eight weeks.

VisiCalc

Software Arts introduces VisiCalc, the first computer spreadsheet program. Initially available only on the Apple II, the program was an instant success. VisiCalc was the first "killer app"—a program so popular that people would buy computers just to run that one program. Customers flocked to ComputerLand and other retailers, asking to see "the VisiCalc Machine."

WordStar

MicroPro International, founded by former IMSAI employees Rob Barnaby and Seymour Rubenstein, introduces WordStar, the first word processor for microcomputers. The predecessor to WordStar, a text editor program called NED, had been developed at IMSAI. IMSAI (and ComputerLand) founder Bill Millard told Barnaby that there was no money to be made in software. Ironically, IMSAI folded the same month that MicroPro opened its doors.

TRS-80 Model I

Radio Shack introduces the TRS-80 model I, the first complete, pre-assembled small computer system. The TRS-80 has Microsoft BASIC built-in, further solidifying Microsoft's grasp on the small but growing computer language business.

BASIC for Apple

Microsoft licenses Microsoft BASIC to Apple Computer, expanding the Microsoft empire beyond the Altair-compatible marketplace.

The Birth of OS/2

IBM and Microsoft announce a new operating system called OS/2 to be jointly developed and marketed by IBM and Microsoft. OS/2 is touted as a next-generation replacement for MS-DOS, but OS/2 will not run on the large installed base of IBM PCs and XTs. Users find the new system too complicated and expensive. Differences over the future of OS/2 eventually lead to a bitter feud between the two companies.

MS-Windows

Microsoft founder Bill Gates announces that Microsoft has begun work on a "integrated windowing environment," first called Interface Manager, then renamed MS-Windows. Early versions of the program are slow and buggy, and the lateness of the project becomes a constant source of embarrassment to Microsoft. Still, Gates keeps Windows a top priority and a personal pet project.

IBM PC

IBM introduces the IBM Personal Computer. Microsoft beats archrival Digital Research to win the lucrative contract to provide the languages and operating system for the IBM machine. Microsoft's PC language compilers include BASIC (built-in), FORTRAN, and COBOL.

Windows 3.0

After seven years of work and three false starts, Microsoft delivers a workable version of Windows. Windows 3.0 and the follow-up Windows 3.1 change the entire software industry overnight. Vendors of popular application programs, caught in a changing marketplace, find themselves struggling to convert their programs to run under Windows. Some leading software vendors, notably Lotus and WordPerfect, drag their feet, and are overtaken by new products from (guess who?) Microsoft.

The Macintosh

Apple Computer's January introduction of the Macintosh splits the software community in two. Smaller software developers must choose between developing software for the Macintosh or the IBM PC. Ironically, this situation helps Microsoft because it is one of a very few companies with enough resources to sustain a large development staff for both Mac and PC programs. By 1987, Microsoft is the largest provider of Macintosh software.

Lotus 1-2-3

Software startup Lotus Development Corporation introduces Lotus 1-2-3, a spreadsheet program designed specifically for the IBM PC. 1-2-3 runs up to 10 times faster than any competing program—including Microsoft's Multiplan, introduced the same year.

1-2-3 did for the IBM PC what VisiCalc had done for the Apple II. Lotus quickly jumped ahead of Microsoft in total software revenue—a position the company held for three years.

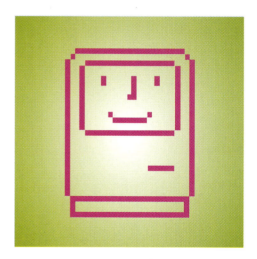

The Macintosh

THE INSTANT SUCCESS of the IBM Personal Computer put Apple in an uncomfortable and unfamiliar position. For the first time in its life, the venerable Apple II faced serious competition. Apple had already begun work on a new computer, code-named Lisa, a year before the introduction of the IBM PC. But Lisa was a long-term, next-generation project, and Apple needed a stopgap product to bolster sagging Apple II sales.

The result was the Apple III. Although it was intended to be a more powerful replacement for the Apple II, Apple promised that the machine would be able to run all existing Apple II programs. The resulting machine was late to market, poorly designed, broke down regularly, and didn't run many Apple II programs. Fortunately for Apple, the Apple III was largely ignored by the buying public, who continued to buy Apple IIs.

Apple's next product was the Lisa. The Lisa was completely different from any product Apple had done before. Inspired by work done at Xerox Corporation's Palo Alto Research Center, the Lisa was a new concept in personal computers. Lisa used Motorola's newest 16-bit microprocessor, the 68000, which was about 10 times as powerful as the Apple II's 6502. Instead of typing commands on a keyboard, users used a pointing device—a mouse—to point to commands on the screen. The Lisa's display screen was graphical, using icons and symbols to represent files, programs, and commands.

The Lisa was also very expensive and confusing to buy. After buyers muddled through myriad combinations of memory size, disk drive, and operating system options, they'd find that a fully-equipped Lisa could top $10,000. The high price put Lisa well out of the reach of the small business buyer—the same buyer who had made Apple so successful in the company's early days. The early Lisas were also plagued by quality control problems, many related to Apple's decision to make their own disk drives.

The Lisa's biggest shortcoming had nothing to do with the hardware, though. Early on in the Lisa project, Apple decided to develop all the Lisa software—a word processor, spreadsheet, database manager, and communications program—by itself. Outside software suppliers like Microsoft and Lotus weren't invited to write software for the Lisa, and Apple did not offer a suite of software development tools to third-party software developers until a year after Lisa's introduction.

Fortunately for Apple, founder Steve Jobs had seen early on that Lisa was going to be a flop, and had begun work on another new machine. Jobs envisioned an "appliance computer" that customers could unpack, plug in, and begin using with little or no computer knowledge.

Like the Lisa, the new machine—the Macintosh—would use a graphical display instead of the text-based display of the Apple II. The Macintosh would also use a mouse, and the Mac's operating system would be designed to ensure that all application programs operated in a similar fashion.

Introduced in January 1984, the Mac was an almost instant success. The early Macintosh machines had their share of problems, but Apple—having learned a tough lesson with the Apple III and Lisa—responded quickly to customer demands. More importantly, Apple had invited 20 software vendors to design programs for the Macintosh, and Apple provided loaner machines and technical assistance to those developers. As a result, a wide range of software was available for the Mac from day one. The Macintosh almost certainly saved Apple from extinction.

The Macintosh is still very much with us today, and Apple has retained their place among the world's top PC makers. Apple weathered the storm caused by IBM's arrival in the small computer business, and Apple once again ships more computers than IBM. Ironically, the newest generation of Macintosh computers use a microprocessor designed and built by IBM.

Evolution of the Macintosh

The Lisa (1983)   The Lisa project began in 1980 and wasn't delivered until 1983. Apple founder Steve Jobs reportedly designed the layout of the machine—with the computer circuitry, video display, and disk drive all in one piece—long before he knew what would go inside the box. When completed, the Lisa used a Motorola 68000 16-bit processor and could accommodate up to 512 kilobytes of memory—a staggering amount at the time.

Like the Macintosh that would succeed it, the Lisa relied heavily on concepts developed by scientists at Xerox Corporation's Palo Alto Research Center. The Lisa display screen was graphical, allowing text and graphic images to be mixed on the same screen. Users executed commands with a then-novel pointing device called a mouse.

The Lisa was never a commercial success, partly because of Apple's refusal to allow third-party companies to develop software for the machine. The machine shown here is a Lisa II, an improved model introduced in 1984. Apple sold quite a few Lisa IIs to software developers, since the only development tools available for the Macintosh ran on the Lisa.

All photos courtesy of Apple Computer, Inc.

1980   1981   1982   1983   **1984**

OK

The Macintosh 128 (1984)

Looking like a Lisa that has been left in the dryer too long, the Macintosh was first introduced to the public in 1984. Like the Lisa, the Mac used a graphical display and a mouse. Unlike the Lisa, the Mac had a reasonable price ($2,495) and was introduced along with a complete suite of software.

The original Mac used the same Motorola 68000 processor as the Lisa, and the machine had a built-in 9-inch monochrome screen. The early Macintosh machines were very slow, owing to their small memory and a slow 400-kilobyte disk drive. Apple responded quickly to customer demands, and a 512-kilobyte "Fat Mac" was introduced less than a year after the original Mac 128.

The Macintosh II (1987)

Keeping with Job's vision of an "appliance computer," the original Macintosh had no internal expansion slots. To keep costs down, the machine was offered with only a monochrome screen. Realizing that color graphics and expansion slots had been two major reasons for the success of the original Apple II, Apple relented and introduced the Macintosh II.

The Macintosh II came in a conventional PC-style case, allowing the buyer to attach a monochrome or color screen as needed. The Mac II also had seven expansion slots, allowing users to install additional video boards, image scanners, and other equipment as their needs required. The Mac II moved the Macintosh firmly into the business marketplace, and variants of the Mac II are still in production today.

Cancel

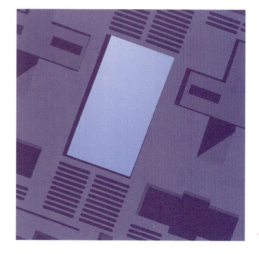

Computing on the Go

THE "PERSONAL COMPUTER" has changed a lot since the early days of the Altair and IMSAI, including in size. A complete Altair system with a disk drive, keyboard, and monitor easily weighed in at over 100 pounds—not something you'd want to take with you on a business trip.

Several companies proposed to build all-in-one-box computers. In 1980, microcomputer pioneer Adam Osborne created the first workable portable computer—modestly named the Osborne I.

Osborne's machine broke new ground in several areas. First, it was truly portable (weighing in at 17 pounds), with a built-in video display, two floppy disk drivers, and a detachable keyboard. But Osborne's biggest innovation was "bundling" software with the hardware. For the base price of $1,795, Osborne included several of the most popular software packages, including a word processor, spreadsheet, database manager, and the BASIC programming language. Early Osborne ads pointed out that the software alone was worth more than the Osborne I's list price.

Osborne Computer Corporation is long gone—one of the many casualties of IBM's entry into the small computer business—but the concept of bundled software is very much with us today. Virtually every computer sold today comes with a suite of software already installed.

As Osborne was fading into the sunset, an upstart computer company in Houston, Texas, was just being born. Compaq Computer Corporation built their success on building the first portable IBM-compatible computer.

Compaq's early success was largely due to a gaping hole in IBM's product line. Although IBM commanded a huge share of the market for desktop personal computers, IBM did not offer a portable. Seeing an opportunity, Compaq's founders decided to market a 100 percent IBM-compatible portable computer.

The first Compaq portable was similar in size and shape to the Osborne I, with a built-in video display and detachable keyboard. Osborne's machine was a compromise, with a tiny 5-inch video screen and slow, low-capacity disk drives. Compaq's designers, on the other hand, cut no corners. Their machine, at 28 pounds, was quite a bit heavier than the Osborne, but the Compaq machines were solid and fast, often providing better performance than IBM's comparable desktop machines.

Compaq sold $111 million worth of computers their first year in business, making them the most successful startup company in the history of American business. Compaq has since expanded into desktop machines, and is now one of the top three computer makers in the world.

Three Views of Portability

In today's competitive marketplace, you can choose from hundreds of different models of portable computers. All of those machines owe a debt in one way or another to the three machines shown here.

The Osborne I (1980)

The first truly portable computer was built by computer book publisher (and shameless self-promoter) Adam Osborne. The Osborne I computer used a Zilog Z-80 microprocessor chip—essentially a faster, better clone of Intel's 8080 chip. The 17-pound Osborne I had no hard disk, but offered two floppy disk drives. Two open slots beneath the disk drives held extra disks, so the user could change disks quickly.

The tiny 5-inch black-and-white screen could only display 52 characters across, but special arrow keys moved the display left and right across a wider "virtual" screen.

For the base price of $1,795, the Osborne I included WordStar (a word processor), SuperCalc (a VisiCalc clone), dBase II (a database manager), and two varieties of the BASIC programming language.

The machine was plagued with reliability problems, but Osborne sold tens of thousands of Osborne I computers. In 1983, the company announced that they would build an IBM-compatible portable, called the Vixen. Buyers immediately stopped buying the Osborne I, waiting instead for the Vixen. Meanwhile, Compaq Computer stepped up to the plate with its IBM-compatible portable computer, and Osborne slipped into bankruptcy. The Vixen was eventually completed and Osborne emerged from bankruptcy, but Compaq had already overtaken the market.

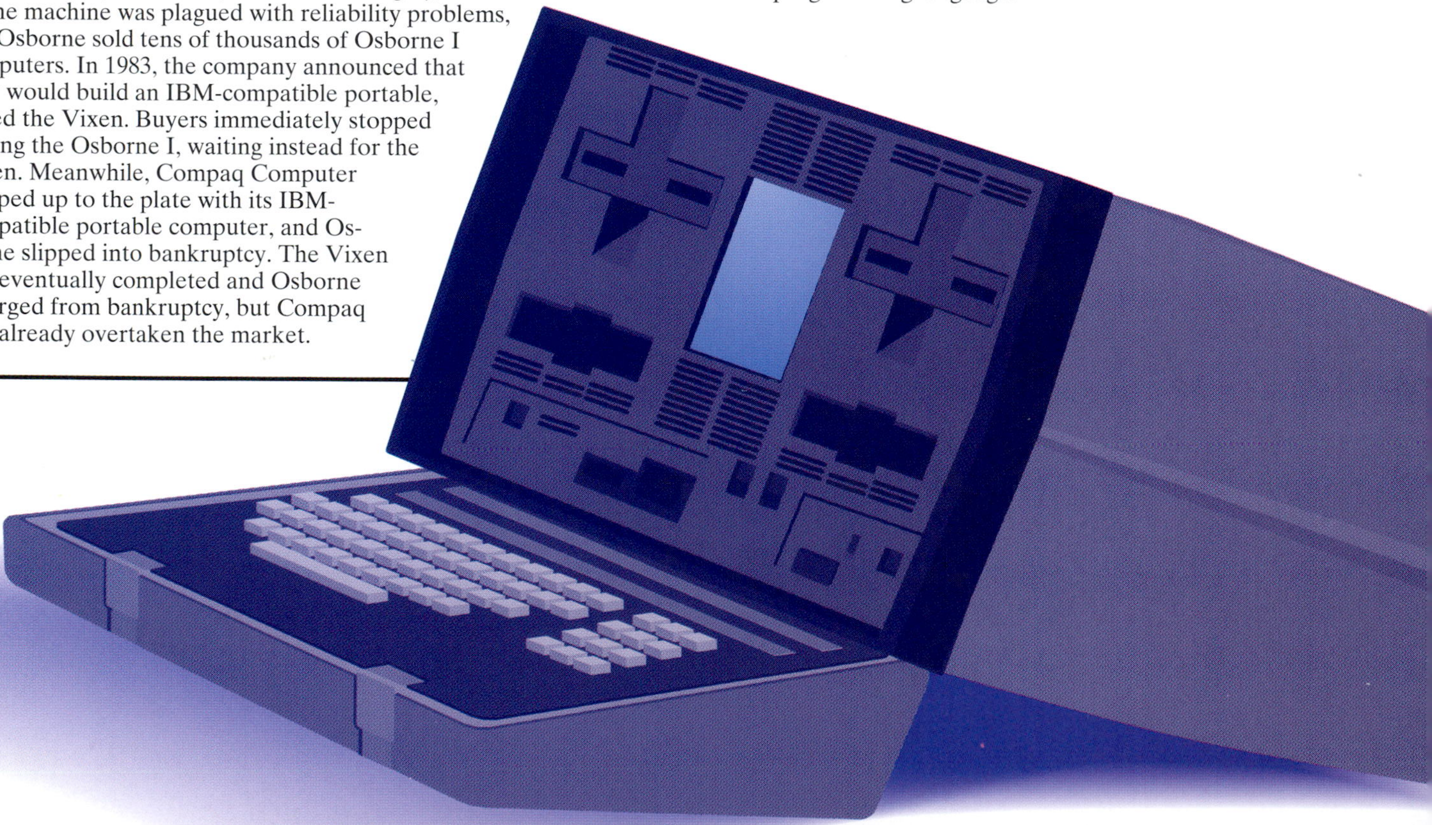

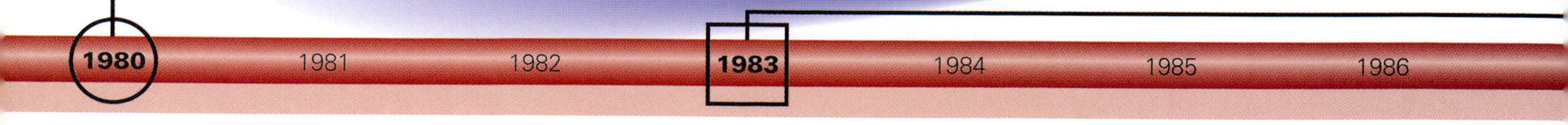

The Compaq Portable Computer (1983) Compaq Computer Corporation stunned the computer world with their 1983 announcement of a portable, 100 percent IBM-compatible portable computer. Several other manufacturers had built "compatible" machines before, but Compaq's was the first IBM-compatible that could start from an IBM diskette—the acid test of IBM compatibility. Other manufacturers had shied away from 100 percent compatibility, fearing a lawsuit from IBM.

Compaq's machine was heavy—the floppy-disk-only model weighed in at 28 pounds. Despite the weight, the Compaq caught on with the traveling computer user, and it soon became common to see business people lugging their "sewing machine" computers through airport terminals and hotel lobbies. Despite its size, the Compaq portable performed well, and even improved on IBM's PC-XT by displaying high-quality text and graphics on the same screen. The Compaq had five expansion slots, allowing the user to add any IBM-compatible expansion card to the machine—further increasing the Compaq's weight but increasing its usefulness.

Apple's PowerBook Series (1991)

In 1991, Apple Computer startled the computer community with the release of a powerful new series of battery-powered portable computers, raising the standard for portables. Several manufacturers (including Apple themselves) offered battery-powered portable computers before the PowerBooks, but Apple was the first to combine a bright, sharp screen, a built-in pointing device, and long battery life in one machine.

For a time, Apple was the largest maker of notebook computers, passing longtime leaders Toshiba and Compaq. Other makers have since adopted many of Apple's innovations and regained market share, but Apple still commands a large share of the compact computer market.

Courtesy of Apple Computer, Inc.

1989   1990   **1991**   1992   1993   1994   1995

Point and Click Computing

N 1981, XEROX CORPORATION unveiled a revolutionary new computer. The Xerox Star introduced the world to a new type of computing. Like many small computers before it, the Star had a built-in video display and a keyboard. But the Star also had something no previous computer had—a little box on wheels called a mouse.

The Star operated differently from most computers. To perform an action on most computers, you entered a series of commands by typing on the keyboard. On the Star, you rolled the mouse around with your hand, which in turn moved a little arrow on the screen. To perform a command, you moved the arrow to the command, and pressed a button on the mouse. Xerox called the Star's method of operation a *graphical user interface*, or GUI.

This all seems old hat today, but in 1981 it was a revolutionary idea. Xerox—whose main business was and still is photocopiers—didn't quite know what to do with the machine. While the Star was very easy to use, it was also very slow. Xerox had chosen Intel's 8085 microprocessor—essentially an updated version of the 8-bit 8080—to power the Star. Several Star systems were installed at the White House and the Pentagon, but the machine was never a commercial success.

Even though Xerox didn't sell many Stars, the machine had a tremendous effect on two very important people. Steve Jobs of Apple and Bill Gates of Microsoft both saw the Star, and both immediately launched projects to bring some elements of the Star's user interface to personal computers.

When Jobs first saw the Star, he was working on the Lisa, Apple's ill-fated successor to the Apple II. Jobs decided that the Lisa would have a graphical user interface. Like the Star before it, the Lisa was also a commercial failure. But the Lisa's failure was due to manufacturing and reliability problems, not its graphical user interface. Apple would finally get it right with the Macintosh, introduced in 1984.

The Macintosh GUI system (known only as "the system" in Macintosh parlance) was an improved version of the GUI that had powered the Lisa. The Mac was a huge success for Apple, saving the company from almost certain extinction. Dozens of software developers—including Microsoft—developed software to take advantage of the Mac's all-graphic operation. Several key application programs, notably Aldus Pagemaker and Microsoft Excel, gave the Mac capabilities not available on any other computer.

Microsoft's path to GUI success on the IBM PC would take a little longer. Bill Gates's vision of a graphical user interface became Microsoft Interface Manager, quickly and thankfully renamed Microsoft Windows. The first version of Windows was shown to the public in 1983. Windows 1.0 was clunky and slow, especially when compared to the sharp graphics and fast operation of the Macintosh. Windows's performance was partially hindered by Gates's decision to make Windows run on any IBM PC-compatible machine. Microsoft worked on Windows on and off for the next seven years, interrupted by an excursion to create a new graphical operating system called OS/2 in conjunction with IBM.

In 1990, Microsoft parted ways with IBM and introduced Windows 3.0, an improved version designed to take advantage of the additional speed and memory power of Intel's 80386 processor. Windows 3.0 took off like a rocket, and at one point Microsoft was shipping several million copies of Windows each month.

Today, virtually all IBM-compatible computers are preinstalled with Windows, and of course all Macintosh computers come with the Macintosh GUI system.

File Options Window Help

Graphical User Interfaces: Point and Click Computing

Most of today's computer users take their computer's graphical user interface for granted. But before the mouse, early computers and PCs used a keyboard-oriented command structure. To use an operating system or application program, users had to remember dozens—even hundreds—of command sequences.

Graphical user interfaces literally changed the face of computing. GUI systems make it possible to learn how to perform a task, such as word processing or page layout, without having to learn much more than a few commands. This simplicity has opened vast new markets for computer hardware and software makers, allowing them to sell computers and programs to a technically unsophisticated user base.

To make it easier for users to learn new programs, both Apple and Microsoft have published guidelines for application software developers. These guidelines spell out (in agonizing detail) exactly how "well-behaved" application programs should work. As a result, users who learn the ins and outs of one program on the Macintosh or in Windows can quickly learn another program.

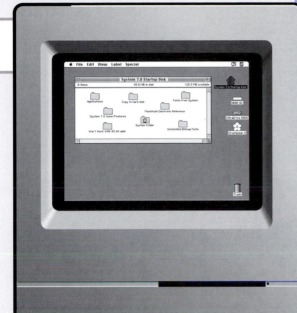

The Macintosh

Apple's Macintosh, introduced in 1984, revolutionized the personal computer industry. The Mac was the first mass-produced personal computer to employ a graphical user interface. Apple capitalized on the Mac's ease of use by marketing the Mac as a computer "For the Rest of Us," thus implying that the IBM PC and other less graphical computers were for nerdy engineer types. Apple's plan worked, and the Mac quickly became one of the most popular computers on the market.

The current release of the Macintosh operating system, System 7, was introduced in 1991. A revised version, System 7.5 (nickname: System seven-and-a-half) was released in 1994. Virtually all Macs run System 7, making it one of the most widely used operating systems in the world.

Microsoft Windows

Microsoft's Windows 3.0, introduced in 1990, quickly became the standard operating environment for Intel-based PCs. The success of Windows 3.0 and later versions is a testament to Microsoft's persistence; the very first version of Windows was released in 1983 but never caught on with users.

Some of this apathy was due to a lack of application programs. Except for Microsoft's own offerings, there were very few programs available for Windows until 1990. Most PC software vendors preferred to put their development efforts into programs for MS-DOS.

Today, virtually all Intel-based PCs come with Windows already installed, and thousands of application programs are available for Windows. The next version of Windows, Windows 95, will combine DOS and Windows into one seamless piece of software. But DOS isn't dead yet—Windows 95 will still run your favorite old DOS programs.

| 1988 | 1989 | **1990** | **1991** | 1992 | 1993 | 1994 | 1995 |

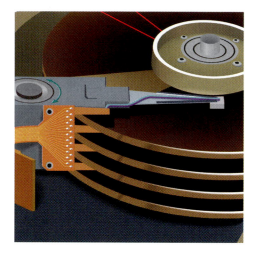

CHAPTER

21

Key Developments

SMALL COMPUTERS HAVE come a very long way since the days of the Altair. Much of the progress in personal computers is due to faster and more powerful microprocessors, but several other key innovations have also contributed to making computers more powerful and useful.

Computer memory technology is one of those key innovations. In the Altair days, random access memory (RAM) chips were very expensive and unreliable. The most popular memory chip at the time provided 2 kilobits (256 bytes) of memory storage in a single 16-pin integrated circuit. To put that in perspective, a modern PC with 16 megabytes of memory would need 65,536 such chips!

Intel, IBM, Hitachi, and other semiconductor makers have made continual improvements to memory chip technology, and RAM chips are now one of the most reliable components in a computer. Besides increasing reliability, chip makers have also increased the storage capacity of RAM chips. One megabyte RAM chips are now common, yet the price of RAM chips has fallen steadily over the years.

Even with one megabyte or more per chip, memory requires a great deal of circuit board "real estate": A typical 16-megabyte PC that uses one megabyte chips would need room for 16 memory chips. Another problem is that memory chips are typically mounted in plug-in sockets to allow for easy upgrading and replacement, but the use of sockets compromises the system's reliability.

Enter the single in-line memory module, or SIMM. A SIMM is a small circuit board with several memory chips permanently attached. The SIMM snaps into a special socket on the computer's main circuit board. One SIMM typically holds nine surface-mount memory chips. SIMMs allow easy memory upgrading and replacement without the reliability problems of chip sockets.

Disk storage is another key component that has come a very long way since the 1970s. The computer history display at the Science Museum in London includes a 20-megabyte disk drive manufactured by English computer maker ICL in the early 1970s. The drive is about 4 feet tall, 5 feet long, and 3 feet wide. In contrast, the 200-megabyte drive in a typical portable computer is 1½ inches tall, 4 inches long, and 3 inches wide, and it holds ten times the data of the museum's monster drive.

Advances in Computer Components

Computers have become more powerful and reliable, yet computer prices keep falling. How is this possible? Economies of scale play an important part, but so do the prices of some key components.

The Single In-line Memory Module

The SIMM, or single in-line memory module, allows fast and easy installation of computer memory. A SIMM is actually several memory chips soldered to a small circuit board. One end of the circuit board is a connector that plugs into a socket on the computer's motherboard (the main circuit board).

SIMMs are more reliable than individual memory chips, and they require less labor to install. The bad news is that if one chip on a SIMM goes bad, you must replace the entire SIMM.

1970   1972   **1973**   1974   1976   1978

The Winchester Hard Disk

Virtually all hard disk drives made today are based on Winchester technology. The Winchester disk was developed by IBM in the early 1970s and uses a set of read/write heads that float above a rapidly rotating rigid metal platter.

The early Winchester disk drives used a single platter with one set of heads. Modern Winchester disks use several platters with multiple heads. This technique increases the capacity and speed of the disk drive.

The CD-ROM

The compact disc read-only memory (CD-ROM) is a variant of the popular compact disc developed by Sony and Philips in the 1970s. A CD-ROM disc holds up to 600 megabytes of data on a $5^1/_4$-inch disk—about as much data as 600 floppy disks can contain.

After a slow start in the mid-1980s, CD-ROM drives have now become standard equipment on most new PCs. The CD-ROM's large storage capacity enables software developers to deliver large amounts of data on a very compact, reliable storage medium.

| 1980 | 1982 | 1984 | 1986 | **1987** | 1988 | 1990 |

Computers Everywhere

WHEN INTEL'S ENGINEERS designed the first microprocessor in 1971, they thought they were building a better calculator. Over 20 years later, we know that their invention changed the world. While the microprocessor gained fame for providing us with cheap and powerful computers, it also became the enabling technology behind many everyday electronic items.

Electronic designers utilize microprocessors in their products for many reasons. A single microprocessor can often do the work of dozens or even hundreds of conventional electronic circuits. Using a microprocessor often cuts down on the number of parts in a device, which in turn reduces manufacturing costs while increasing reliability. Some consumer electronic items simply wouldn't exist without the microprocessor. Fax machines, digital satellite receivers, and home video games all rely on microprocessors to make them work.

Microprocessors have also caused a revolution in navigational technology. A new navigation system called the Global Positioning System (GPS) is the first navigational system to provide accurate, worldwide position information. GPS uses a group of 24 satellites. Each GPS satellite transmits a precisely timed beacon signal. Back on Earth, GPS receivers pick up signals from several satellites at once. A microprocessor inside the GPS receiver compares the timing differences between the signals and computes the receiver's position. GPS receivers are small (about the size of a paperback book) and extremely accurate. GPS technology brings accurate, no-brainer navigation within the reach of almost every boater and pilot.

Computers now play an increasingly important role in medicine, too. The Computerized Axial Tomography (CAT) scan has become an important diagnostic tool. The CAT scan uses a computer-controlled x-ray beam to produce a highly detailed cross-sectional image of any part of the body. A CAT scan can show minute details not visible with conventional x-ray methods, while exposing the patient to a much lower level of radiation than a conventional x-ray.

Federal mandates have forced automobile makers to find new ways to improve fuel economy while reducing exhaust emissions. Auto makers have turned to microprocessor technology to help solve these problems. Virtually all new cars now use a microprocessor-based engine control computer system. These systems monitor key engine operating conditions, and automatically adjust the engine to keep it operating at peak efficiency over a wide range of conditions. Auto makers have also used microprocessors in creating new safety features like antilock brakes (which have electronic sensors that can tell if a wheel is skidding and adjust the brakes to compensate) and air bags (which have an electronic system for sensing when to deploy an air bag).

In a way, the microprocessor can even take credit for the downfall of the Soviet Union. For many years, the Soviet government kept a tight lid on information flowing in and out of the USSR. The Soviet security agency, the KGB, routinely monitored telephone conversations and mail, watching for subversive activity. The arrival of fax machines and modems in the early 1980s signaled the start of a new era. For the first time, people were free to exchange ideas and information outside the watchful eyes and ears of the KGB.

The Digital Satellite System

Until recently, having a satellite dish meant having a 10-foot or larger monster dish in your yard or on your roof. A new type of satellite system called Digital Satellite System (DSS) has changed all that.

DSS uses computer technology to bring several hundred channels of television into your home via an 18-inch dish antenna. Unlike other satellite systems, DSS is all digital. Program providers like HBO and CNN transmit their picture and sound to a central location called the uplink center. A computer at the uplink center converts the analog picture and sound into digital data. The computer also combines the data from all the services into one large data stream, using sophisticated data compression technology. The data is transmitted up to the satellite, 22,300 miles above the Earth. The program provider authorization center processes statements for bills. DSS is linked to the customer service center by means of the phone jack on the back of your DSS receiver.

Uplink Center

CNN

HBO

The DSS satellite dish collects the satellite's coded program information and relays it to the DSS receiver.

The satellite relays the digital data back down to Earth, where it is received by a small dish antenna at your home. A microprocessor inside the satellite receiver separates the various channels from the data stream and converts the data back into a conventional analog picture that you can watch on your TV. Because the data is digitally coded, DSS pictures are free from interference caused by atmospheric noise, lightning, and other electromagnetic disturbances.

With conventional satellite systems, users must adjust the position of the receiving dish to receive signals from several different satellites. Switching channels takes time, since the dish must be rotated to point to the desired satellite. Because all the DSS channels are on one satellite, DSS systems use a fixed dish, allowing users to "channel surf" at will.

If your TV has a remote control, you can program the DSS universal TV remote to change channels and volume.

DSS receiver

The DSS TV universal remote controls the DSS system as well as most remote-controllable TVs, VCRs, and other devices.

Cut Here

Cut Her

PLEASE TAPE HERE ONLY—DO NOT STAPLE

6. What is your level of experience with personal computers? With the subject of this book?

	With PCs	With subject of book
Beginner.	☐ -1 (24)	☐ -1 (25)
Intermediate.	☐ -2	☐ -2
Advanced.	☐ -3	☐ -3

7. Which of the following best describes your job title?

Officer (CEO/President/VP/owner). . . . . ☐ -1 (26)
Director/head. . . . . ☐ -2
Manager/supervisor. . . . . ☐ -3
Administration/staff. . . . .☐ -4
Teacher/educator/trainer. . . . . ☐ -5
Lawyer/doctor/medical professional. . . . .☐ -6
Engineer/technician. ☐ -7
Consultant. . . . . ☐ -8
Not employed/student/retired. . . . . ☐ -9
Other (Please specify): _____ ☐ -0

8. What is your age?

Under 20. . . . . ☐ -1 (27)
21-29. . . . . ☐ -2
30-39. . . . . ☐ -3
40-49. . . . . ☐ -4
50-59. . . . . ☐ -5
60 or over. . . . . ☐ -6

9. Are you:

Male. . . . . ☐ -1 (28)
Female. . . . . ☐ -2

Thank you for your assistance with this important information! Please write your address below to receive our free catalog.

Name: _____

Address: _____

City/State/Zip: _____

Fold here to mail.

2753-16-19

Ziff-Davis Press Survey of Readers

Please help us in our effort to produce the best books on personal computing.
For your assistance, we would be pleased to send you a FREE catalog
featuring the complete line of Ziff-Davis Press books.

1. How did you first learn about this book?

Recommended by a friend . . . . ☐ -1 (5)

Recommended by store personnel . . . . ☐ -2

Saw in Ziff-Davis Press catalog . . . . ☐ -3

Received advertisement in the mail . . . . ☐ -4

Saw the book on bookshelf at store . . . . ☐ -5

Read book review in: _____ ☐ -6

Saw an advertisement in: _____ ☐ -7

Other (Please specify): _____ ☐ -8

2. Which THREE of the following factors most influenced your decision to purchase this book? (Please check up to THREE.)

Front or back cover information on book . . . ☐ -1 (6)

Logo of magazine affiliated with book . . . . . . ☐ -2

Special approach to the content . . . . ☐ -3

Completeness of content . . . . ☐ -4

Author's reputation. ☐ -5

Publisher's reputation . . . . ☐ -6

Book cover design or layout . . . . ☐ -7

Index or table of contents of book . . . . ☐ -8

Price of book . . . . ☐ -9

Special effects, graphics, illustrations . . . . . . ☐ -0

Other (Please specify): _____ ☐ -x

3. How many computer books have you purchased in the last six months? _____ (7-10)

4. On a scale of 1 to 5, where 5 is excellent, 4 is above average, 3 is average, 2 is below average, and 1 is poor, please rate each of the following aspects of this book below. (Please circle your answer.)

Depth/completeness of coverage	5	4	3	2	1	(11)
Organization of material	5	4	3	2	1	(12)
Ease of finding topic	5	4	3	2	1	(13)
Special features/time saving tips	5	4	3	2	1	(14)
Appropriate level of writing	5	4	3	2	1	(15)
Usefulness of table of contents	5	4	3	2	1	(16)
Usefulness of index	5	4	3	2	1	(17)
Usefulness of accompanying disk	5	4	3	2	1	(18)
Usefulness of illustrations/graphics	5	4	3	2	1	(19)
Cover design and attractiveness	5	4	3	2	1	(20)
Overall design and layout of book	5	4	3	2	1	(21)
Overall satisfaction with book	5	4	3	2	1	(22)

5. Which of the following computer publications do you read regularly; that is, 3 out of 4 issues?

Byte . . . . ☐ -1 (23)

Computer Shopper . . . . ☐ -2

Corporate Computing . . . . ☐ -3

Dr. Dobb's Journal . . . . ☐ -4

LAN Magazine . . . . ☐ -5

MacWEEK . . . . ☐ -6

MacUser . . . . ☐ -7

PC Computing . . . . ☐ -8

PC Magazine . . . . ☐ -9

PC WEEK . . . . ☐ -0

Windows Sources . . . . ☐ -x

Other (Please specify): _____ ☐ -y

Please turn page.

Imagination
INNOVATION·INSIGHT

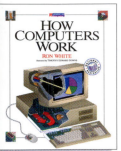

HOW COMPUTERS WORK
RON WHITE

ISBN: 094-7   Price: $22.95
Also available in Spanish.

No other books bring computer technology to life like the HOW IT WORKS series from Ziff-Davis Press. Lavish, full-color illustrations and lucid text from some of the world's top computer commentators make HOW IT WORKS books an exciting way to explore the inner workings of PC technology.

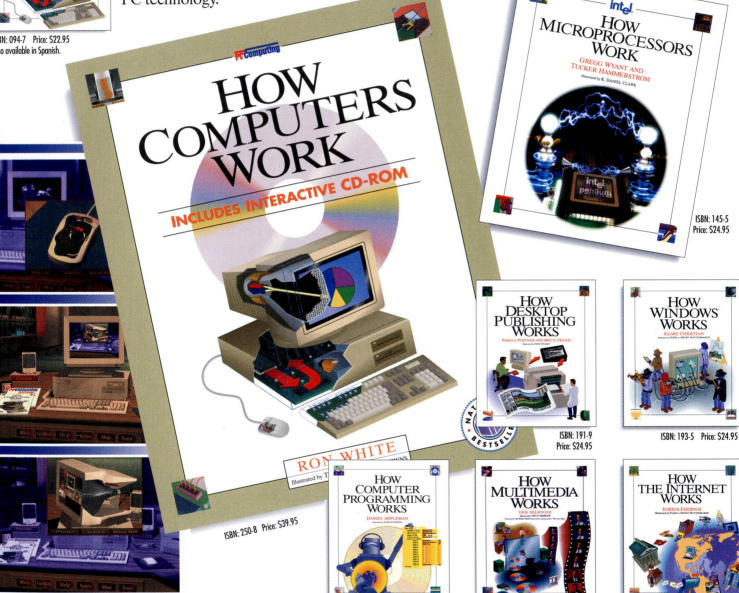

PC Computing

HOW COMPUTERS WORK

INCLUDES INTERACTIVE CD-ROM

RON WHITE
Illustrated by T...

ISBN: 250-8   Price: $39.95

intel
HOW MICROPROCESSORS WORK

GREGG WYANT AND TUCKER HAMMERSTROM
Illustrated by K. DANIEL CLARK

ISBN: 145-5
Price: $24.95

HOW DESKTOP PUBLISHING WORKS
PAMELA PFIFFNER AND BRUCE FRASER
Illustrated by DAVE FEASEY

ISBN: 191-9
Price: $24.95

HOW WINDOWS WORKS
KAARE CHRISTIAN
Illustrated by PAMELA DRURY WATTENMAKER

ISBN: 193-5   Price: $24.95

HOW COMPUTER PROGRAMMING WORKS
DANIEL APPLEMAN
Illustrated by SARAH ISHIDA

ISBN: 195-1   Price: $24.95

HOW MULTIMEDIA WORKS
ERIK HOLSINGER
Illustrated by KEVIN BERGER

ISBN: 208-7   Price: $24.95

HOW THE INTERNET WORKS
JOSHUA EDDINGS
Illustrated by PAMELA DRURY WATTENMAKER

ISBN: 192-7   Price: $24.95

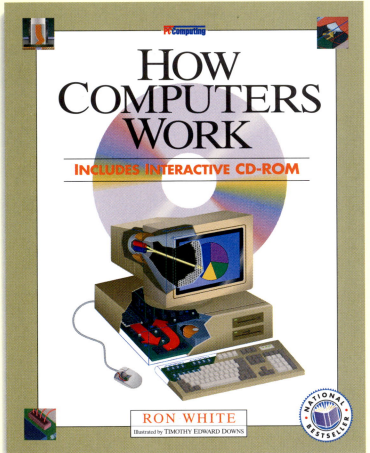